clean mama's guide to a peaceful home

clean mama's

GUIDE TO A

peaceful home

EFFORTLESS SYSTEMS AND JOYFUL

RITUALS FOR A CALM, COZY HOME

BECKY RAPINCHUK

HarperOne
An Imprint of HarperCollins Publishers

HarperCollins books may be purchased for educational, business, or sales promotional use. For information, please email the Special Markets Department at SPsales@harpercollins.com.

FIRST EDITION

Designed by Janet Evans-Scanlon
House with trees image by Elvetica/Shutterstock
Clean Mama branding and icons by Spruce Rd.

Library of Congress Cataloging-in-Publication Data has been applied for.

ISBN 978-0-06-299612-1

20 21 22 23 24 LSC 10 9 8 7 6 5 4 3 2 1

To my family, home is anywhere you are

CONTENTS

A Simple Shift Toward Less Stress and More Joy Inside Our Homes

Life can feel overwhelming.

Every single day we're barraged with millions of decisions to make—everything from how often to hit the snooze button to how to handle a conflict at work. Even something as simple as picking up milk at the store has turned into a complex process with dozens of options where once there was one.

It's too much. Our brains were not designed to handle the onslaught of stimuli that comes with our hyperconnected world, and our bodies were not designed to handle the stress of an increasingly demanding, frenetic pace. And while home should be the one place we can go to find peace and quiet—our sanctuary in the storm—too often we feel stressed and overwhelmed when we get there.

At our house, for example, managing the dishes is a constant source of conflict. At the beginning and end of a busy day, the last thing anyone wants to do is load or unload the dishwasher! As someone who loves a good organized checklist and routine, I know there must be a way to make this task easier. A way that taking care of my home doesn't have to be yet another chore but could actually put my mind at ease and perhaps, just perhaps, even be a bit enjoyable.

Because isn't that what we're ultimately after? Creating a home that feels peaceful? Making it a space for conversation and games and connection with those we love?

I want you to love your home again. So much so that I want this book to be a love letter to your home. Let's look at how to stop feeling overwhelmed and put some practices in place to turn your home into a haven.

Systems + Rituals

How can we possibly simplify our lives and protect our limited energy? How can we save our mental and physical resources for what matters when we're constantly overloaded with what doesn't? I've found that it comes down to implementing two simple things: systems and rituals.

By definition, according to the Merriam-Webster dictionary, a system is an "organized or established procedure" and/or a "harmonious arrangement or pattern," while a ritual is "an act or series of acts regularly repeated in a set precise manner." Depending on your personality and the current state of your home, these definitions either make you more or less excited to read this book. Spoiler alert: systems and rituals can make the little things in life more enjoyable, even chores and tasks that you have previously disliked. If you think about it for a minute, you'll realize that life is full of systems and rituals—eating meals, answering emails and texts, brushing your teeth, getting dressed, signaling before you turn your car, washing your hands before eating, putting clothes in the dryer after they come out of the washer. All these systems and behaviors are learned: some are taught when we are young, some we learn by observing other people, but most of the time, we figure out what works for ourselves through trial and error.

What if these systems weren't a chore but came with a little something that we enjoyed? Would that make the system work a little better? Would tasks be easier to complete? More enjoyable? Easier to remember? Systems are the salve our souls need in a chaotic world. They free us from the mundane and trivial so we can focus our time and energy on what really matters.

What if you reframed your thinking and regarded your home as a blessing and place of refuge regardless of its imperfect, non-social-media-worthy appearance? Comfortable, cozy—not a house but a home. Reframing the way you view your home and how it works for you and your loved ones will change how you feel about it and how you treat it. Even when you're tired, even when you don't know where to start, even when you're embarrassed to open the doors to welcome a friend or neighbor. Finding systems that work and pairing them with rituals is what has clicked for me. It's about taking time to slow down and enjoy even the big and small details.

Attaching a ritual to a system not only helps us remember to do it but also brings a little happiness to it. Is it fun to clean a bathroom? Probably not, but if you use products you love, such as cleansers with pleasant scents that don't give you a headache, and if you have a system for getting it done quickly, you are rewarded with clean bathrooms. Is it fun to change the sheets? Not really, but when you feel that crisp, clean sheet on your skin and smell the lavender linen spray on your pillows when you finally settle in after a long day, you appreciate the effort you made.

Chances are you already have some systems in place in your home. Perhaps when your kids enter the house, they know they should take their shoes off. You might need to give them some reminders at first, but after a while, they don't even think about it—they just kick off their sneakers at the door. But in the constant churn of daily life, it can feel almost impossible to press pause and set up systems for *everything* you do in your home. And how will you know what works and what doesn't? You probably don't have the time, energy, or inclination to set up a system, then tweak and repeat it until it works flawlessly.

That's where *Clean Mama's Guide to a Peaceful Home* can help.

I'm going to walk you through your home and help you identify the Pain Points and trouble spots that are begging for a less complex, more intuitive system. I'll share simple solutions that have worked in my home while allowing you to identify your own specific needs and goals so that you can customize your processes to suit the way you live.

As we cover each area of the home, you'll find spots where you can jot down what your Pain Points are, as well as beautifully illustrated decision trees that will guide you, step-by-step, to finding the best solution for your problems.

But setting up systems is about more than productivity. It's about making space—both physical and mental—for things you actually *enjoy* doing. I know it sounds counter-intuitive, but we all have certain tasks we don't mind doing around the house. Maybe it's watering the plants, loading the dishwasher just right, or chopping fresh vegetables. Whatever those tasks are—and they're different for everybody!—those are your rituals.

Rituals are the tasks that can bring you to a place of calm concentration, almost momentary Zen, if you perform them with the right tools and the right mind-set. After all, even our most enjoyable tasks can feel stressful if we're rushed, don't have a proper work space, or can't achieve a positive frame of mind.

Which is where systems come back in. When we put the two together, we get something new: systems + rituals = bliss. As I discuss the various areas of the home, I'll help you differentiate between your Pain Point Tasks and your Happy Tasks so you can better understand how to manage each. Your Pain Point Tasks will get solved by systems, so you no longer have to think about them and they'll get done as quickly, efficiently, and painlessly as possible. Your Happy Tasks will become your rituals, and I'll help you find the space, time, and energy to squeeze every drop of enjoyment out of them.

Ultimately, my goal is to help you find joy in what you love and effortlessness in what you don't. It's about building the kind of invisible framework that can support the weight of daily life. This framework—this structure of systems and rituals—gives our days a natural rhythm and adds a new kind of freedom to our lives. Most important, it transforms our homes from just another chaotic space into a peaceful oasis where we can anchor ourselves and our families, safe from the storms of daily life.

Instead of going to the place where you feel overwhelmed by all the work ahead of you, I want to encourage you to start with a positive mind-set, one in which you see this as a process that will make your home run smoothly and help you find a slow, sustained rhythm that works. The goal isn't to reach perfection: your only task is to find the best way of doing what needs to be done for your home and family. I've intentionally organized the chapters so that they correspond to sections of the house. Instead of looking at your whole home at once, start by looking at individual rooms, drawers, corners, areas. By shortening your focus and looking a little more closely, you'll find a way to make a simple routine out of what you're already doing.

Small steps matter, and establishing rhythms around the mundane can make life more meaningful, because these rhythms slow our pace while simplifying everyday life. We feel rushed, busy, overworked, and overscheduled at every turn. What if we could halt that pace at home? Let's automate the things that suck time away from us and put that time back into our days. Let's return to a pace that slows us down and allows us to enjoy life. Even if everything else is moving at breakneck speed, we are in control of the pace at home. Let's embrace simple and slow.

Can You Really Change a Habit?

Before we go further, I'm going to be honest with you: you need to decide that moving forward is important to you. Finding your way to a streamlined home, systems that work, and rituals that you enjoy doing will take some work. There are probably a handful of reasons—or a hundred—why you've been putting these things off. Reasons why the clutter has built up or why you just aren't taking the minutes each day it would take to reach your goals. I'm guessing your reasons are something like this: too busy, too tired, too many kids, kids are too young, someone is sick, you just want to sit down and relax, you don't like taking care of your home, the tasks feel old-fashioned, no one helps, what's the point if it just gets messy again, and so on.

If you are reading this, chances are you want things to be different. You're looking for more calm, peace, quiet, organization, order, coziness, cleanliness. I want you to have those things, and it's easier than you think it is. You can change your habits, but make sure you're ready to make the little changes that are necessary—they're going to add up to big changes before you know it.

If you've been trying to get into a routine or habit or make some sort of change and it hasn't happened, but you continue to try with the same results, let's just assume that's not the way this is going to work for you. For example, let's say you want to organize your family photos, and this has been on your to-do list for years. Back up and ask yourself why you aren't getting the photo organizing done. Is it a lack of time, effort, energy? Try to break down that goal a different way—split it up, make it less overwhelming. Maybe you can put goals down on paper, set a timer on your phone, or come up with a reward for yourself. Whatever gets you excited to try this thing that you need or want to do, approach it that way and see if you don't have a different outcome.

As you think about adopting a new habit, try to reframe that new habit as a system or a ritual. Don't get me wrong: habits can be good, but they can also be bad. I'm sure you can think of more bad habits than good, so let's think of how we can move ourselves forward positively with systems and rituals. Doesn't that sound much better? "I have a system for that" or "That's a favorite ritual for me" instead of "I have a habit of unloading the dishwasher" or "I have a habit of making coffee in the morning." See the difference?

If your system has been to just move through life and take care of things as they come, or to clean in a fury before guests stop by or when the dust bunnies become unbearable, you can change this system. The change won't take place overnight, but with little steps, the consistency will pay off in big ways. I promise! Even the worst home habits can be changed and turned into systems and rituals to make your home a place that is welcoming, relaxing, and cozy.

Did you know that we make more than thirty-five thousand decisions every day? Thirty-five thousand decisions, most of which we don't consider or spend time on. Decisions that are just refined habits carried out by practice and repetition. Checking your email, locking your car when you leave it, closing the door after entering, turning a light off when you leave the room. Did you contemplate whether to take those actions? Or did you simply act out of habit? Sure, there was a learning curve and a time when you did think about what to do and when to do it, but now these decisions are on autopilot.

Can you put other things in your life on autopilot like this? Are there things that you just wish you did without a lot of thought and trouble? Of course there are! Everyone has a different level of routine—and systems and rituals—in the home.

If you're feeling like things are out of control, and you cannot fathom where, let alone how, to start, you most likely don't have a sufficient number of systems in place. If you feel like this book is just what you need to up your game at home and enjoy homekeeping even more, you might have many systems already in place. Regardless of your starting point, this book is for you. What works for you might not work for your sister or best friend or your children, but there's a little bit of fun in figuring out what will work and what won't. Even when you think you have it all figured out, something will change and you'll need to take another look at that system that was working so well. Go slow, take your time, and enjoy the process.

Is It Possible to Love Cleaning and Homekeeping?

Have you ever had any of the following thoughts during a chaotic time or when your house feels cluttered? *Burn it down; throw everything away; I'd rather just get rid of everything.* If so, this book is for you. If you've ever thought, *I should have a system for that* or *There has to be a better way of doing things*, this book is for you. If cleaning and organizing feel like one big horrible chore, this book is also for you.

Keeping a home shouldn't be difficult; it should be *enjoyable.* I truly believe that pairing systems with rituals can bring simplification, focus, and a different sort of routine that improves the way your home functions for you.

I wrote this book to encourage you, and my hope is that it brings real, lasting change into your home. This isn't for someone who already "has it all figured out." I might be someone who enjoys cleaning and homekeeping, but that doesn't mean I can't relate to what you're going through. I want you to know that I have been in just about every homekeeping scenario, and I know where you're coming from. I also don't want you to feel like you have to spend money in order to pair systems with rituals in your home. It's a mindset—you already have everything you need; you just need to figure out the best ways to make these things work in your home. You can do this in a one-bedroom apartment, a studio apartment you can't wait to leave, a rental home you don't love, a town house you can't wait to sell, your parents' basement, the bedroom you rent, a two-story home that feels like a burden, or the home of your dreams. This is a process for every home and every heart. It's time to stop longing for something you don't have: it's time to find contentment where you are. Believe it or not, systems and rituals are meant to help you find your way there.

Is there something that has been holding you back from getting started on your home? A lack of time, a lack of energy, an idea in your head of what a perfect home looks like? Write down a couple of things that come to mind here, or save this space for ideas that come to you as you read on.

First up? Let's identify and talk about the things we love doing and the things we hate doing. Hold these in your mind as you read and work your way through *Clean Mama's Guide to a Peaceful Home*. Remember that this is about reframing your mind-set when it comes to homekeeping: it's about putting systems and rituals in place so that you'll enjoy your home because it will work for you rather than you working for it.

finding time
and
creating routines

CHAPTER 1

What Kind of Home Do You Want?

BEFORE WE TOUCH A SINGLE ITEM IN OUR HOMES, WE'RE GOING TO CONDUCT a thought experiment. I want you to start by taking a deep breath. The important thing here is that you are becoming aware of the type of home environment you want to create and the ways your current home is or isn't meeting that ideal.

Think of a home you've been in that made you feel especially warm and cozy. Or think of a feeling you've had in your present home that you want to re-create. For example, when I was growing up, any time we cooked or baked, the old leaded glass windows in the kitchen would steam up. I loved that contrast between the warm kitchen and cold windows. That felt like home to me. Now that I am a homeowner, I understand what it means—the windows were old, with inefficient heat retention—but the image brings back warm memories of baking Christmas cookies on a cold Wisconsin weekend in a cozy stone home.

Do you have a memory from a childhood home—maybe yours, maybe your grandparents', maybe a friend's—that conjures up feelings of love and safety? What made it special? What feelings do you want to create in your current home?

Those feelings and memories are important, because we all know they're what make a house a home. And although some special moments just happen spontaneously, we can control the factors that enable us to re-create these moments with the people in-side our homes.

Make a list of five to ten things that make you feel good about being in your home. These could include a clean bathroom, the feel of fluffy bath towels, the aroma of a favorite candle or scent diffuser, a vase of flowers you grabbed on your weekly grocery store run, kitchen counters without stacks of papers on them, a closet filled with clothes that fit, a toy room where toys are played with and put away, a garage you can park a car in, a book on the nightstand you have time to read.

Now make a list of five to ten things that make things complicated at home. These could be things such as having more coats than hooks to hang them on, piles of mail on the counter, backpacks scattered on the floor, shoes left on the steps, toys without a place to store them.

Make a list of a few ways you want others to feel when they are in your home, such as welcomed, loved, and comfortable.

_____

_____

_____

_____

I'm guessing that the things on your lists have nothing to do with the size of your home, how old the carpet is, or whether you cleaned your bathroom this morning. When you slow down, when you notice and appreciate the space you're in, when you refine your systems and take the time to work on things that will make your home feel and function better, when you repeat what works and edit out what doesn't, you'll find your sweet spot. Isn't that refreshing? Slow down, appreciate the home and life you have, and fine-tune your systems and rituals as we turn those Pain Point Tasks into Happy Tasks.

CHAPTER 2

Pain Point Tasks
and
Happy Tasks

DO YOU HAVE TASKS THAT YOU PUT OFF BECAUSE YOU REALLY DON'T LIKE doing them? You know, the chores you let pile up and dread even more because they turn into bigger piles or bigger jobs than they have to be? These are Pain Point Tasks. Maybe they take too much time, feel inconvenient, or meet you with resistance for some reason. These Pain Point Tasks are different for every person. My dreaded Pain Point Task is loading and unloading the dishwasher. I just don't like this task! For some people it's vacuuming; for others it's folding laundry; for others it's dealing with all the paperwork that accumulates at home.

The opposite of Pain Point Tasks are Happy Tasks. These are tasks that you enjoy completing, give you a sense of accomplishment or satisfaction, and make you a little happier. It's important to recognize that some tasks hold us back because we don't enjoy them while others we don't mind or even like doing. There might be someone reading this book who *enjoys* unloading the dishwasher (who knew?). Once you take a good look at all the systems you have in place and evaluate whether and how they're working for you, you can pair your systems with your rituals and find your bliss.

Once we recognize that both Pain Point Tasks and Happy Tasks exist in our lives, we can put them together and change the way we incorporate them into our days. It isn't always easy to see how to merge these tasks, but they complement each other and make the mundane a little more enjoyable.

Let's start with an example that goes back to the early years of my marriage, when my husband and I were comparing notes and discussing ways to do things around the house.

As I mentioned, loading and unloading the dishwasher has always been a Pain Point Task for me. I know that we are blessed to have a dishwasher, and I am so thankful that I have one, but unloading and loading it is not a Happy Task for me. I used to dread it (I still kind of do) and put it off as long as I possibly could. I'd have a stack of dishes on the counter waiting to be washed. I'd painstakingly (not an exaggeration) unload the dishwasher, then subsequently load it up. This process took more time than it should have because I hated doing it and had created more work for myself by putting it off.

Years ago, my husband asked me why I was doing the dishes this way. I took offense at his observation and said because I hate doing the dishes and loading the dishwasher. He (accurately) pointed out that if I would unload the dishwasher as soon as it was done running, I could just put the dirty dishes in the empty dishwasher throughout the day and the counter would be clear.

At the time, I definitely didn't let him know that he had a point, but it made sense to me, and I decided to give the process some thought and try it. For this to work, it needed to take less time. I was already unloading and loading as quickly as I could, so the only other way to make it easier was to divide the task into two phases as my husband suggested. So the next day I unloaded the dishwasher before breakfast, and surprisingly, when the breakfast dishes could go right into the dishwasher, loading it seemed less daunting. There was also room in the dishwasher to load the dirty lunch and dinner dishes as soon as the meals were finished. Though this system didn't instantly make me enjoy the task, it did make it a little easier.

The unloading-and-loading process became easier as I repeated it every morning. I also noticed that I could start and finish this task in the couple of minutes that it took for the coffee to brew. Then it clicked—I started to pair these two things together for success. Start the coffee, unload the dishwasher, then enjoy the coffee! I still don't love unloading the dishwasher, but I don't mind it now that it doesn't take so long. Besides, racing the coffeemaker gets me moving a little more quickly in the morning! It also feels good to sit down with that cup of coffee in front of a clean, empty dishwasher that's ready to be filled instead waiting to be unloaded later.

Think about tasks that you don't like, forget to do, or put off unnecessarily. Sometimes pairing them with a task you enjoy or don't mind is what makes the undesirable task become a good habit.

List your three biggest Pain Point Tasks—the tasks you dislike the most.

List your three favorite Happy Tasks—the tasks that you enjoy completing or at least find a little satisfaction in when they're done. If you don't have any Happy Tasks yet, don't worry—you'll have some very soon.

Do any of your Pain Point Tasks and Happy Tasks intersect? Are they carried out in the same room of your home? Could they be done at the same time to make the Pain Point Tasks a little easier to accomplish or less dreadful? Write down an idea or two for merging them here.

Come back to this space and write down other Pain Point Tasks and Happy Tasks as you're reading this book and working through your home. You don't need to do anything with them right away, but jotting them down as you go will help make those Pain Point Tasks a little less painful.

PAIN POINT TASKS	HAPPY TASKS

Now that we've started to understand which tasks are challenging and which bring joy, let's take a close look at our schedules and find the time to start putting these routines and systems into place!

CHAPTER 3

Finding the Time

IF YOU HAVE CONSISTENTLY TRIED AND FAILED TO MAKE CHANGES TO YOUR homekeeping routine in the past, chances are you might have determined that you just don't have the time or you are too busy to start something new. But creating a system or a ritual doesn't take all that much time—perhaps thirty minutes to start—and once it becomes a habit, it often takes very little time or mental energy to accomplish.

Still, I know we all are overscheduled and overtired and don't think we can fit one more thing into an already packed calendar. So let's start by taking a look at what's filling our days, hours, and minutes. Many things are necessary and crucial, such as work, sleep, and time with your family. But there are also a lot of things that distract us throughout the day. I think you'll find that you are so much more productive when you take control over your distractions and pull back from things that fall outside your priorities.

Time Log

An easy way to see where you're spending your time is to make a time log. It's basically just a simple way to see at a glance where you're spending your time. First, take a week to jot down what you're doing at various points during the day. I like to use a highlighter and color-code various tasks so I can see a little more quickly where my time is being spent.

Time Tracker

today's date:

❧	TASK	❧	TASK
6:00 am		2:00 pm	
6:30 am		2:30 pm	
7:00 am		3:00 pm	
7:30 am		3:30 pm	
8:00 am		4:00 pm	
8:30 am		4:30 pm	
9:00 am		5:00 pm	
9:30 am		5:30 pm	
10:00 am		6:00 pm	
10:30 am		6:30 pm	
11:00 am		7:00 pm	
11:30 am		7:30 pm	
12:00 pm		8:00 pm	
12:30 pm		8:30 pm	
1:00 pm		9:00 pm	
1:30 pm		9:30 pm	

Streamline Your Phone

Our phones often gobble up more of our time than we realize! By streamlining what we access on our phones, we can take control of our time. Look at your social media and unfollow or delete accounts that make you feel bad about your home or your life. Below are some tips that will help you start.

- Unfriend friends who aren't really your friends.

- Delete any apps that you don't use (they're cluttering up your phone).

- If there are apps that you want to keep but don't want on your home screen, move them to another screen to hide them temporarily. Or create a folder on your phone for apps that you're thinking of getting rid of, place them there, and if you haven't used them within a span of time (say, a few months), delete them. You can always download apps again if you need them.

- Update your wallpaper and lock screen. A solid-color background (aqua for me) is my favorite kind of wallpaper. It feels less cluttered and makes it easy to see apps at a glance.

Detox from Your Devices

Following are a few things you can do to keep your screen time to a minimum and max-imize your productivity.

- Keep your to-do list on paper.

- Remove email apps from your phone if you can.

- Keep your calendar on paper.

- Turn off phone notifications.

- Designate a specific time for checking email.

- Limit your apps, and set time limits on them to get reminders to set the phone down.

- Stop checking your phone while you're trying to work. Lock it up and put it away.

- Set a physical timer for tasks, and don't use your phone as a timer.

Figure out what works for you and use these techniques to limit your screen time. I think you'll find that you're much more productive when you're *not* multitasking. I know you have at least a little bit of time you can spare for yourself and for your home. Is this time something you want to make use of in your own life? Write down a few thoughts below.

Now go back to your log. What did it tell you about how you're spending your time? Were there any surprises? Are there any pockets of time you want to use differently? Maybe you realized that you spend more time than you'd like watching *The Bachelor* or binge-watching shows on Netflix that you've already seen. (Or am I the only one who does that?) Maybe "checking in on Instagram" is taking an hour every night instead of fifteen minutes. A time log isn't meant to make you feel guilty; it's supposed to help you understand how you spend your time. There's no shame here, just a little awareness. Write down what you learned by going over your time log below.

_____

_____

_____

_____

Can you think of any boundaries you want to establish while you're working through this book? If you're not sure what kind of boundaries you might need, maybe you could start with things like keeping your phone out of your bedroom, not picking up your phone before you've had your morning coffee, turning off your phone during quiet time or time with your kids, and other practices you want to initiate after you looked at your time log. Write down your new boundaries below.

_____

_____

_____

_____

CHAPTER 4

Putting Routines to Work for You

ONCE YOU HAVE A SENSE OF HOW YOUR TIME IS BEING SPENT, YOU CAN PUT structures in place to make the best use of that time. These structures are simply routines.

This probably won't surprise you, but I am a big routine person—I love routine, thrive on it, and function so much better when I follow it. Am I a routine person by nature? Probably. But the reality is that I like knowing what comes next in an unpredictable world. There's so much we can't control, including simple things such as knowing how long a commute will take, knowing how long I'll have to wait in line at the post office, and knowing whether I'll succumb to the stomach flu that's been going through the house. There's not much I can do about these things. I'm sure you can make your own list of things you can't control, but instead of dwelling on that, let's figure out what we *can* control by building a little predictability into our days. When we know what to expect, things run more smoothly and being at home becomes more comforting, more enjoyable, and less frantic.

If you're new to the idea of a routine or tend to think of yourself as someone who is free-spirited and unstructured, putting routines into place might sound boring or robotic or old-fashioned. If that's you, I'll ask that you just stick with me and keep reading. You know the phrase "Don't knock it until you try it"? Adopt that mind-set as you read these pages. Absorb the thoughts and ideas and think about how they just might work for you.

Many times what holds us back from adding a little structure to our lives is thinking that because something hasn't worked in the past, it won't work now. But what if the approach you tried previously just didn't work for your needs or personality or the season you were in back when you tried it? There *is* a way to find structure and love it even if you don't thrive on it. Forget those misconceptions and all the things you thought had to be a certain way because that's what you've always done or that's how you grew up or that's just how it is. This is the time to embrace routine because of what it can do for you and your family. Stop making excuses—you *can* be a routine person. You don't have to be an overachiever to follow a routine, and it might not be something you've done before, but the good news is that it's a learned behavior, and we're going to figure out how to make it work for your specific personality and your home.

Don't think of a home routine as rigid: think of it as a love letter to your home and family. You're spending a little time and energy to get things set up so the things you can control go well. For example, making sure there's a place to drop shoes, coats, and backpacks and having a snack ready for the kids to grab and a clear workspace stocked with pencils and any other supplies they might need to do their homework is a much nicer way to welcome kids home than leaving them to dump their shoes and backpacks wherever they can and search high and low for a pencil before they can do their homework. Providing a nutritious snack also helps refuel them for homework and other after-school activities. This proactive approach can only happen when we are intentional about our time and invest it up front so things go smoothly during the day. And what do you know? Sometimes a Pain Point Task (homework) is paired with a Happy Task (a yummy snack), and just like that, homework isn't quite so bad.

The Daily Routine

Instead of trying to formulate a daily routine out of thin air, we're going to start with three well-established times during the day and build out from there: morning, midday, and evening. Most of our days are already structured around these time blocks—for example, we wake up in the morning, we eat lunch at midday, we get kids ready for bed at night. Whether you like it or not, there's already some sort of routine built into those three times of the day.

Reflect on the routines you have in place during each of these time blocks, then think about what you'd like them to look like instead. As you move through the book, you can come back to this page and figure out what you can pair with them to make the day run more smoothly and to find a little solace in the time you have at home. Are mornings especially frantic? Does everything fall apart in the afternoon? Are you so exhausted in the evening that you lose motivation? It's going to be helpful to use these times of day as benchmarks or starting points for establishing routines because they are most likely already marked by certain patterns.

At this point, we're going to simply evaluate what is and isn't working in your current routines.

First write down the time of day that generally needs some tweaking.

Then ask yourself, Why is this time of day such a struggle?

THE MORNING ROUTINE

Whether you're a morning person or not, this is where your days start. We all know the feeling of leaving the house late, frantic and harried, rushing off to school or work. Wouldn't it be nice if we could set our mornings up so that we could get out the door smoothly?

Let's start by assessing your morning routine. Write down your current morning routine from start to finish.

What is working in your morning routine?

What isn't working in your morning routine?

_____

_____

_____

_____

What is your ideal morning routine?

_____

_____

_____

_____

It's important to note that as much as I love and recommend structure and routine, I understand that I can never get _too_ rigid in my routine because every day needs a little flexibility and grace to change with life and schedules. But following is an example of my current routine as I would love it to be on a perfect day, when everything aligns.

- Wake up between 4:30 and 5:00 a.m. I am a morning person and enjoy being up early because the house is dark and quiet and I am alone. (If the idea of being up before the sun makes you want to dive back under your comforter, then get up later! This is about finding what works for you.)

- Take care of the dogs. We have two Weimaraners who get up with me, and they demand my attention to be fed and taken out. A couple scoops of food, filling their water bowls, and a trip outside makes them happy, and then they settle in where they know I'll be in a couple minutes.

- Unload dishwasher + make coffee (this is a paired Pain Point Task + Happy Task).

- Read and spend time with my devotional and my coffee.

- Check in on emails and schedule my workday. (I work from home and don't love answering emails in the morning because emails can sway the direction of the day. I am trying to move checking email to the afternoon, but old habits die hard!)

- Go for a walk or work out before the kids are up. (My husband gives them breakfast and helps them get ready for school.) I set out my workout clothes the night before to make sure this daily ritual is met with the least resistance.

- Get back from working out around 6:45 a.m. and help the kids make lunches. Put breakfast dishes in the dishwasher.

- Supervise the kids' morning routines—make sure rooms get at least a little tidy and teeth get brushed.

- Get the kids out the door for the bus—everyone is gone by 8:00 a.m.

- Shower and get ready for the day.

- Do a quick bathroom cleanup—this consists of putting toiletries away, making sure towels are hung up to dry, sinks are wiped if necessary, and toilets are flushed. (Kids! ☺)

- Start a load or two of laundry.

- Do a daily or weekly cleaning task (see chapter 5).

- Head to my home office and start working around 8:30 or 9:00 a.m.

I am able to get quite a bit done in the early hours before the rest of the family is up, and I love having this time to myself. It also means that I can spend after-school and evening hours with my kids and husband.

Some people just aren't morning people and are going to get their tasks done later in the day or at night. But I hear all the time about people who wish they *could* be morning people! If that's you and you want to get up earlier but aren't sure how, I have a few ideas to get you started.

- **Start the evening before.** The key to success in the morning is setting yourself up the evening before. I recommend cleaning the kitchen at night, because that's one of the things that makes getting up early a little easier. Why? You won't have to wake up to a mess from the day before—you've already reset your kitchen. This is a huge help in keeping up a routine because you aren't waking up to work. Who wants to do that? You're waking up to something that will make your day run more smoothly.

- **Turn off the screens.** Turning off phones and computers and televisions is the best way to get yourself ready for bed. Stop sleeping with your phone— the electromagnetic fields mess with your natural body rhythms. We keep our phones and devices downstairs in a charging station. I find that putting them away early in the evening (in a perfect world, before dinner) is really helpful. Get a cute old-fashioned alarm clock and use that instead of your phone.

- **Go to bed when you're tired.** Stop fighting through the tiredness and just go to bed. If you're used to staying up late, try going to bed earlier and see how you feel. See if it makes a difference in your day. Everyone needs to sleep, but everyone's perfect amount of sleep is different. Make your goal six to eight hours and experiment to find what makes you feel most rested and alert during the day.

- **Get your morning drink going.** Coffee, lemon water, a smoothie, tea—whatever you drink first thing in the morning, get that going as soon as possible. It gives you something to look forward to when you step out of bed. I like to start my coffee as I'm unloading the dishwasher and make it a race to see who wins—me or the coffee machine. You might find that getting a pitcher of lemon water ready the night before is just what you need. Or maybe your coffee machine has a timer on it so you can set it up the night before and waltz into the kitchen just as the last drop hits the pot.

- **Start small.** If you want to get up at 5:00 a.m. but are currently getting up at 7:00 a.m., don't just jump into the two-hour time difference. Set your alarm for 6:00 or 6:30 a.m. for a week or so and go to bed earlier. When you're ready to make the adjustment to 5:00 a.m., work backwards in fifteen- to thirty-minute increments over the course of a week or even a month. If you like the results, keep going to bed a little earlier and waking up earlier until you've formed this habit. You might find that getting up at 6:00 a.m. gives you plenty of time and you aren't interested in getting up any earlier.

THE MIDDAY RESET

There aren't as many routines built into the midday hours, but everyone can benefit from a midday reset. It's the perfect time to evaluate your day and see how it's going. Tweak what needs tweaking. Take a break, clean something up, go for a walk, eat lunch. Whatever you need to do to keep moving is what will be most helpful.

When the kids were little I did a reset every day between lunch and nap or rest time. Some days we went for a stroller walk, some days we went to the park, other days we turned on music and played a cleanup game. Whether you're at home or work, try to do some sort of midday reset to refresh and recharge.

Write down your current midday routine from start to finish.

_____

_____

_____

_____

What is working in your midday routine?

_____

_____

_____

_____

What isn't working in your midday routine?

_____

_____

_____

_____

What is your ideal midday reset?

_____

_____

_____

_____

Below is what my current midday reset looks like.

- Take a break around 11:30 a.m.

- Make and eat lunch. I usually make a big salad or have leftovers, but whatever it is, I sit down and eat it somewhere other than my office. Sometimes I'll take it outside; other times I'll read a book or magazine while I eat in the kitchen or watch part of a movie or television show I'm into. I try to fully take a break from work to get the benefits of a midday reset.

- Go for a walk or play with the dogs outside so they get some exercise.

- Do a little dinner prep if necessary.

- If I didn't do my daily or weekly cleaning task in the morning, I'll usually do it before I go back to my home office. If not, I'll save it until around 4:00 p.m., after all the kids are home and while they're doing homework or playing.

- Head back to my office by 12:30 or 1:00 p.m. and work until 2:00 or 2:30, when my youngest comes home from school.

Below are some ideas for tweaking your midday routine.

- If you frequently feel like you can't take a break to eat lunch, switch tasks while you're eating. If you've been at the computer all morning, for example, step away from it and read a book or write in your journal or planner. Get up from your desk to get your lunch, even if you have to bring it back to your desk. Physically leaving your workspace can help clear your head.

- If you sometimes forget to eat lunch, set a timer on your phone or computer to remind yourself.

- If you rarely get outside during the day, try to take a quick walk before or after lunch. Listen to a podcast or just walk and listen to nothing and clear your head. If you have little ones, let them eat lunch in the stroller while you walk.

- A midday reset can also be a good time to check in with your planner to see what you still want to get done before too much of the day is over. Move anything you can't do today to the day after so you can focus on the current day's most important tasks.

THE EVENING ROUTINE

Depending on your schedule, your evening routine might start when you get home from work, when you get dinner on the table, or when it's time for bed. I'm going to encourage you to think of your evening routine as something that starts when you begin to get dinner ready. This is an event you can count on, and it will make it easier for you to draw a line from start to finish.

In my family, the evening routine starts around 5:00 p.m., when the kids are mostly done with homework and playing outside or in the house. Sometimes we're finishing up sports practice or heading out to one, but on most nights, the clock for getting dinner ready begins ticking around 5:00 p.m. We're usually all seated at the table and eating by 6:00 p.m.

My evening routine wraps up with a kitchen reset (see page 72), and once that's done, we turn down the overhead lights—I love the cozy look and feel that the under-the-counter lights give to the kitchen. We'll usually have a candle burning or diffuser running in the evening to give the first floor of the house a little ambience. Then the kids finish up their homework and take their showers. After that, we might play a game, watch a show on TV, or read books before heading to bed. The kids are usually all tucked in around 8:00 or 8:30, and my husband and I head upstairs around 9:30 p.m.

Write down your current evening routine from start to finish.

_____

_____

_____

_____

What is working in your evening routine?

_____

_____

_____

_____

What isn't working in your evening routine?

_____

_____

_____

_____

What is your ideal evening routine?

_____

_____

_____

_____

Below are some ideas for tweaking your evening routine.

- If you want to get more sleep, try powering down your devices and TV before you go to bed. Reading something in print, even if it's just for ten minutes, will help you wind down and form a new habit.

- Before bed, take a bath, make a cup of tea, or do something that feels restorative. This will fill you back up with reserves of energy for the next day. Find pockets of time that you can use for yourself.

- Start making changes to your routine one night a week, rather than all at once, and see how that feels. Add new habits as you are able to—you don't have to take a bath every night or make a cup of tea every night, but maybe that feels good on Monday nights. Start there.

The next step is to use the space below to consolidate what you'd like your morning, midday, and evening routines to look like. Be realistic, but dream about how you want these three times of the day to look and feel. As I'm writing this, I'm making a couple of notes to myself about ways I want to adjust my own routines in the new year. In doing so, I find that I want more family time, less work time, and more time for reading and outdoor activity.

Here's your chance for change: write down your ideas and try them out one at a time. Even if you implement just one or two new habits, that's a win.

My New Morning Routine

_____

_____

_____

My New Midday Reset

_____

_____

_____

My New Evening Routine

_____

_____

_____

You don't need to do anything with these routines yet, but now that they're on paper you can refer back to them, refine them, and strategically implement them in your home life as you go forward.

The Weekly Routine

Feeling motivated to go a little further? Write down your weekly schedule. For example, if you work Mondays and Tuesdays and are off Wednesdays, make a note of that. Maybe your daughter takes dance lessons on Saturday mornings and your son has soccer on Thursday evenings and Saturday afternoons. Write down whatever is set in stone.

CURRENT WEEKLY SCHEDULE

Monday

Tuesday

Wednesday

Thursday

Friday

Saturday

Sunday

Look at the schedule you've written—is there anything you can or want to remove? You don't have to do everything. Let's pause and evaluate: maybe you can drop a committee membership or some other activity that feels like it's a bit too much.

Now let's dream about your ideal weekly schedule. The point is not to be overbooked; the point is to do less by setting priorities and boundaries, which will free you up for rest, spontaneous moments with your kids, and catchall tasks at home. Go ahead—what is your dream weekly schedule? Jot it down on the following pages.

IDEAL WEEKLY SCHEDULE

Monday

Tuesday

Wednesday

Thursday

Friday

Saturday

Sunday

Next, write down three things you need to do to achieve that ideal weekly schedule:

Remember, there's no pressure at this point to reconfigure your entire daily and weekly schedule all at once. What I want to show you is that making your home work for you is as much a shift in mind-set as it is a shift in action.

Put a bookmark or a sticky note on page 33 and come back to it after you've set up your systems. I bet you'll be ready to implement your ideal weekly schedule sooner than you think!

CHAPTER 5

A Clean-Home Routine
for Any Schedule

IF YOU FOLLOW ME ONLINE, YOU KNOW THAT MY SIMPLE DAILY AND WEEKLY routines are the foundation of the Clean Mama Routine. I live with my husband, three children, and two dogs, so this isn't all about me, but we have some basic routines that help us keep our stuff together and truly enjoy life.

I have seen how a simple cleaning routine, implemented little by little, can change even the most disorganized and cluttered home. It's all about pairing your tasks with joyful rituals that help you get those tasks done. Below is a quick overview of the way this simple cleaning routine works. Don't be concerned with putting a brand-new cleaning routine in place along with everything else we're working through in this book: these ideas are intended to help you find your way to a clean home gradually as we move forward.

Five Daily Tasks

The following five daily tasks are the secret to a clean home most of the time. Proactive home care is much more effective than reactive home care. It's about what you and your family can do daily to make things run more smoothly. These tasks take just minutes a day, and with a little effort you'll soon find that they can be life changing.

- **Make beds.** Quickly pull up your bedding and fluff those pillows as soon as you can in the morning. This will help your mind-set for the day. I prefer to forgo a top sheet and just use a bottom sheet and a washable duvet cover or quilt. Just quickly pull the duvet or quilt up, toss the pillows on top, and move on. This is especially helpful for little ones when they are old enough to make their own beds. Even if you don't see your bed again until it's time to climb back into it, you'll appreciate that the bed you finally get to crawl into is made.

- **Check floors.** Sweep or vacuum as needed, but if you can't, try to at least check the floors daily. In my house, it seems like the broom comes out after every meal, but it's just for a quick sweep under the kitchen table, then it's put away. If the day is a busy one, I might overlook the floor until after dinner and only drag out the broom once. If you have pets, you might need to grab that vacuum cleaner or broom a little more often, especially if it's shedding season—or maybe your furry friend can be helpful by picking up the remnants of meals. This is a great little job for kids to take on. Teach them how to use a broom and dustpan and/or a small vacuum cleaner.

- **Wipe counters.** Wipe down your kitchen counters after meals and at least once daily after dinner. I include emptying and loading the dishwasher in the morning in my own mental "wipe counters" checklist. Check the bathroom counters to make sure they're clean and cleared off daily, too. If you keep makeup and beauty supplies out, consider putting them in a basket or drawer so the counters will be clear and easy to clean. A quick walk through the bathroom(s) in your home with a cleaning cloth and an all-purpose cleanser works. Keeping the counters wiped down daily makes it easier to maintain a clean home, and it discourages clutter in the meantime.

- **Declutter.** Dealing with clutter is the number one daily task in our house. I'll be discussing clutter and decluttering quite a bit throughout the book, but I find that coping with it daily is the best way to avoid the overwhelming dismay that comes from seeing a pile of papers on the kitchen counter or a pile of shoes at the door. Adopt a mantra that works for your home when it comes to clutter: touch it only once; never leave a room without putting something away; sort mail daily; put clothes away daily; everything has a place.

- **Do laundry.** I am easily overwhelmed by laundry and find it easier to do one load from start to finish each day than to save it all up for a weekly marathon. Simplify your laundry routine by using just the basics—no need for an arsenal of laundry supplies. Pare it down to a couple of favorites and keep those stocked. My must-haves for fresh, clean clothes? Powdered detergent, white vinegar (for use as a softener), and wool dryer balls to help the clothes dry quickly and eliminate static.

Weekly Tasks

Daily and weekly tasks are what keep our home humming. Completed separately, they will help keep your home clean, but when they're completed together, you'll see even better results. Everyone's busy, and no one really wants to spend more time than necessary cleaning toilets or doing laundry.

MONDAY: BATHROOM CLEANING DAY

Every Monday I clean bathrooms. I don't wash the floors because I wash them on Thursdays—I find that separating these tasks really cuts down on bathroom cleaning time. I also like to keep my bathroom cleaning supplies in each bathroom, but you might prefer to tote a cleaning bucket or caddy from bathroom to bathroom.

You'll need the following supplies for a well-stocked bathroom caddy.

- Disinfecting cleaner—don't forget that hydrogen peroxide works as a disinfectant!

- Window + mirror cleaner

- Toilet cleaner and brush—oxygen-based laundry whitener works great as a toilet scrub (sprinkle, let sit, scrub, flush)

- Microfiber window-cleaning cloth

- 3+ microfiber cleaning cloths for *each* bathroom (1 for counters, 1 for tub and/or shower, 1 for toilet)

- Basket for dirty cleaning cloths—I put the microfiber cleaning cloths in a stainless steel basket in my cleaning closet when I'm done cleaning the bathrooms. This helps them to dry thoroughly. I launder them as their own load when I have a basketful. Microfiber should only be laundered with microfiber and without fabric softener, so keeping it separated from the start is helpful!

Follow this quick method for speed-cleaning your bathrooms:

- Clean mirror

- Thoroughly spray sink, toilet, and tub and/or shower

- Move on to the next bathroom—repeat the first two steps and continue until you've sprayed each bathroom

- Go back to the first bathroom—wipe each surface and scrub toilet

- Repeat wiping and scrubbing in each subsequent bathroom

TUESDAY: DUSTING DAY

I do my best to display only those things that we love and need on our shelves. Especially because I have little kids, I keep a minimal amount of "stuff" out in the open so I don't have to worry about anything happening to it. And having uncluttered surfaces makes dusting so much easier. Weekly dusting makes it simple to keep up with the endless dust that accumulates as part of daily life.

My preference for dusting is to use microfiber cloths and a microfiber dusting wand or dusting mitt. I also use a telescopic duster for cobwebs and hard-to-reach ceilings and corners. After dusting, I use a natural beeswax cream to polish and condition some furniture, either monthly or as needed.

The best way to dust? Work from the top floor down and quickly go through the house, dusting all the hard surfaces, the staircase and railings, the TVs and furniture. When you're doing your weekly dusting, move quickly and do what you can in fifteen minutes. If you have extra time, add a deep-clean dusting with polish or fit in some of your rotating cleaning tasks, such as dusting light fixtures or ceiling fans. If you're just starting out and can't remember the last time you dusted, dust one or two rooms the first week, one or two rooms the second week, and continue until you've dusted everything. Then dust half the house one week and the other half the next week. Pretty soon you'll be ready to dust weekly. As you're dusting and moving things around you might want to have a "donate" bin handy so you can give some of those knickknacks a second life somewhere else.

WEDNESDAY: VACUUMING DAY

Wednesday is vacuuming day, also known as the day to clean up the dust from Tuesday. Move quickly: start on the top floor, with the room that's farthest away from the stairs. If you have a one-level home, start at the corner farthest from the front door. Vacuum bedrooms, bathrooms, hallways, stairs, and then the lowest level. The main goal of vacuuming is to get the dust and dirt out of your home by doing a thorough job once a week. Sweep or vacuum in between as needed, but a weekly vacuuming ensures that all the dust and pet hair is picked up and the floors are ready for washing the next day.

THURSDAY: FLOOR WASHING DAY

I wash the floors on Thursdays because they were vacuumed or swept on Wednesday. Yes, it would be better to vacuum and wash the floors on the same day, but I just don't have that kind of time, and I'm guessing you probably don't, either. So let's just split up the task and vacuum on Wednesdays and wash on Thursdays. Alternatively, you can vacuum and wash one floor or section of the house on Wednesday and the other on Thursday. The point is to make sure that your floors are clean by the end of the day on Thursday.

There are so many floor-cleaning products and tools on the market—buy only what fits your budget and what you will enjoy using. I recommend using those that have removable microfiber mop heads or pads. If you like making your own cleaners or want to control what goes into your household products, choose one with a refillable tank so you can load it with whatever you want.

What's the best way to wash hard-surface floors? Start at the corner farthest from the door and wash from left to right until you wash yourself out of the room. Rinse your mop head or microfiber pad frequently to avoid streaking and cloudy floors. Use your favorite tools and floor-cleaning products and work as quickly as you can. If you do, you'll find that you're able to get this often dreaded task done painlessly. If washing the floors weekly is a little hard for you to keep up with, you can tackle one section of the house one week and another section of the house the next week. For example, wash the bathroom and kitchen floors one week and the upstairs floors the next. Don't be afraid to experiment to discover what works with your schedule and cleaning style.

FRIDAY: CATCH-ALL DAY

I designate Friday as my catch-all day. It's a day to work on just about anything homekeeping-related that needs to be tackled before the weekend. Depending on the day and week, I use Fridays to get caught up on uncompleted tasks, menu planning, bill paying, laundry, a deep-cleaning task, or if I'm caught up, I reward myself by taking the day off. You'll find that the weekend is so much more enjoyable if you're truly relaxing and not thinking about any nagging chores and cleaning that you "should" be doing.

SATURDAY: SHEETS AND TOWELS DAY

Saturday is sheets and towels day. I find that doing a couple of loads of sheets and towels on Saturdays helps lighten the laundry load during the other days of the week. Wash a load or two of towels and a load or two of sheets. I find that if I start right away in the morning, by early afternoon clean sheets are on the beds and clean towels are folded and put away. It isn't a nonstop Saturday of laundry: I just tend to the laundry when it needs to be switched from the washer to the dryer and then from the dryer to the folding table and into the closets.

SUNDAY: JUST THE DAILY TASKS

Sunday is a day of rest at our house, and I love that there aren't any weekly cleaning tasks to complete on those days. I do my daily tasks—make the beds, check the floors, wipe the counters, clear clutter—and one load of laundry, plus a little planning for the upcoming week, but that's it. Relax and enjoy your Sunday—do things that refresh you and get you ready for the week ahead. On Sunday evening, if you need to do a little preweek prepping, by all means do it. You'll feel refreshed and ready when Monday comes.

These daily and weekly tasks keep a home running smoothly, and they allow for the unexpected by taking the guesswork out of what needs to be cleaned. For more about my cleaning routine, see chapter 20 as well as my website, CleanMama.com. The complete Clean Mama routine has four parts, two of which we've covered—Daily Tasks and Weekly Tasks—along with Rotating Tasks (deep cleaning) and a Monthly Focus (choosing an area of the home to organize based on the month). If you're ready for more, come on over to the website and check it out.

What is your cleaning routine? Do you have one? Is this something you might want to focus on? Write down your thoughts about a cleaning routine below.

CHAPTER 6

The Clean Mama Declutter Process

MY FAVORITE WAY TO KICK OFF A NEW PROJECT? DECLUTTERING. DECLUTTER-ing frees you from "stuff," and regardless of your clutter level, you'll see progress right away. Yes, sometimes it gets messy before it all comes together, but in my system, clutter doesn't stick around for long. You'll refer back to this section as we go through each and every space in your home, creating systems and rituals to guide your days and simplify your life.

Did you know that clutter can actually cause stress? Eliminate surface clutter, and you'll be ready to find other areas to concentrate on in your home. A quick start will help motivate you to create successful systems and rituals, resulting in bliss.

You don't need to buy anything in order to declutter. Use what you have on hand and get started right away. As you move through this book, follow the process below for each space.

- Create a clutter station. Tag four receptacles (these can be boxes, bags, laundry baskets, or whatever you have on hand) with the following labels.

Keep—Love it, need it, or use it

Toss—Recycle or trash it

Relocate—Still love it, need it, or use it, but it doesn't belong here

Donate—Don't love it, need it, or use it, but someone else could

- Completely empty the space. Regardless of whether the space you're decluttering is a box, a closet, an entire room, or a drawer, remove everything from it *first*.

- Think quickly as you sort through your items. Think about the space you have and what you want it to look like when you're done. Do you really need x, y, or z to move forward in life? Or can you let it go?

- Put everything into one of the four categories. Once everything is sorted into keep, toss, relocate, and donate receptacles, toss what can be tossed, relocate what can be relocated, and put the items to be donated in a bin or bag for a trip to your favorite donation center.

- Wipe down any surfaces and vacuum if necessary.

- Arrange the items you want to keep. Do this in a way that makes sense for your home and space, then admire your transformation!

Decluttering can be complicated, and it most definitely won't be done overnight. Give yourself grace and time to work through the process. We'll continue talking about clutter throughout the book, but you'll also be setting up systems and rituals designed to keep the clutter from returning permanently. Come back to this simple process anytime you need a reset or a little help getting started. Don't get discouraged because you think your house isn't ready, or because you don't have a whole weekend to devote to it, or because you just aren't "there" yet. You can get a lot accomplished in ten-minute increments every day. That time adds up to over an hour a week: don't put decluttering off because you think you don't have time.

Start with a Quick Declutter

Let's start this adventure the way I always start when I feel overwhelmed—with a quick declutter. This will give you a little jump start and ensure that you move through the mess and get to the other side—a simplified space—as quickly as possible. Set your sights on a doable outcome with expectations of feeling better and seeing progress instead of thinking that you'll end up with a completely clutter-free home.

A quick once-over through your home with three garbage bags is all you need to get started. The goal? Fill up the bags with stuff you can toss or donate and gain a little momentum in the decluttering department. Once you have this momentum, you'll be ready to tackle another task.

When can you do a quick declutter? Anytime! Grab three bags, put on some upbeat music, set a timer for fifteen minutes, and methodically move through every room in your home. When I say "methodically," I mean quickly, efficiently, and without giving the stuff too much thought. You're not separating these items into four categories (keep, toss, relocate, donate); you're only concentrating on two categories—toss and donate. This is purposeful, to get the stuff out of your way. Once your timer goes off or your bags are filled up, whichever comes first, move those bags to the garbage can or to a donation area (your car or a holding spot for donations).

A quick declutter is my secret to a clean and less cluttered home: master this method and you'll be able to move through the mess quickly and not get caught up in it. I do a quick declutter daily as part of my cleaning routine and taught my kids and husband to do it, too.

I find that it's best to do a quick declutter before or after something that's already in the schedule, such as a meal. When our kids were little, for example, we did a quick cleanup before nap time. Remember midday routines (page 24)? Decluttering became a great one for us. We'd set a timer for five minutes and declutter the area that the kids were playing in, then they would eat lunch and took their naps. This allowed me to relax or work while they rested and meant that the house was picked up before the next round of playtime. Building this habit around another habit makes it easy to remember, and the kids knew it was coming every single day.

When I was an art teacher, we always spent the last five minutes of class cleaning up so each class could have the same experience as the one before it. Building this habit into something that was already routine was key to its success and left no surprises for the kids. They knew when we did our pickup and expected it.

Pair this quick declutter system with a ritual—such as mealtime, nap time, or bedtime—and you'll start to see it happening daily without the usual effort.

Sometimes, focusing on decluttering methods and habits feels good because you're making tangible progress and clearing junk out of the house, but you aren't dealing with the core problem. It's like chopping down a weed versus pulling it up by the root. Revise the system that's in place, and the clutter won't return.

Not all methods for decluttering are created equal, and one size doesn't fit all. My process is simple, and it works with a busy life (and kids). As much as I'd love to be able to empty an entire room or gather up all our clothes in one big pile and decide what to keep, that's not realistic for me or our family. I work in small chunks of time, with a timer, and with small goals in mind. An organized home is a process, and if you want to do it yourself or with your family members without the help of professionals (wouldn't that be nice?), this is the most foolproof method there is because it takes into account all the things that can derail and halt your progress. It also allows you to pick up where you left off. Making strides but need to go pick the kids up from school? No problem. Came down with the cold everyone else has? You can continue when you feel better. It's a process,

DECLUTTERING WITH KIDS

You might be at the point where you'd rather wait until the kids are grown up and out of the house before you deal with clutter. Or maybe you feel like it's an uphill, losing battle. I know it's not easy. I can honestly tell you that when you say you can't declutter when kids are around, I get it. I know it's difficult, and I know it's hard to wrap your mind around going through stuff with little ones. There's the emotional attachment to stuff and the fact that your kids need your undivided attention, not to mention the fact that you're utterly exhausted. But every minute you put into decluttering is worth it. You'll feel better. You'll be ready to tackle the day and the week. And you'll be able to find stuff quickly, especially the special, important items. Following are tips for decluttering with kids at every age.

Tips for Decluttering with Babies

Nap time is a great time for getting things done, but if you have a *little*, little one, take care of that baby and rest when you can. Focus on small decluttering projects you can do when they're content in the baby swing, carrier, or bouncer, such as sorting through photos, clothing, drawers, and cabinets.

Tips for Decluttering with Toddlers

If you're up for it, use nap time and early bedtimes for decluttering. When you're upending an entire space, focused time where little hands aren't there to get into small objects is key. If you want to tackle some decluttering while they're up, occupy them with something that holds their attention and work in fifteen-minute increments. When my two kids were three and one, I would do a quick cleanup before lunchtime or nap time and then again before dinnertime or bedtime. I'd set the timer for three to five minutes, put on some dance music, and see how quickly we could pick up. This daily maintenance really helped us keep things clutter-free and

continued

got us in the habit of putting things away when we're done.

Tips for Involving Kids (Ages 4+)

In my opinion, getting kids involved is not only helpful for you but good for them, too. That way they're more likely to not get into stuff and dump out that basket of blocks you just went through. Need some ideas for activities that can occupy kids for more than five minutes? Have them sort and group something that you are decluttering. You can also give them a baby wipe to follow you with while you're cleaning, and ask them to wipe doors, handles, and baseboards in the rooms you're working in.

Get a Clutter Partner

If you're struggling with decluttering while kids are around, consider hiring a sitter. Better yet, find someone who wants to declutter, too, and trade kid time. You send your kids over to your clutter partner's house for an afternoon while you work on your clutter, then you switch.

How to Help Kids Learn to Declutter

For the toys that your kids have outgrown or don't play with, suggest packing them up for a younger sibling or donating them to a local charity or preschool. If you want to do this without your kids knowing it, put the items in a bag, and if they don't ask for them for a week or two, it's probably safe to say they won't miss them. I don't necessarily agree with this approach for everything, but there are some items it works with. I also keep a bin in the kids' rooms where we put clothes that they've outgrown. This typically happens when they put on a shirt or pants and find that suddenly the item is too small—I tell them to put it in the "pack away" bin and choose a different outfit. Once the bin is filled up, it's either given to a cousin or put in the basement for a younger sibling or donation.

and by tackling it yourself and/or with family members, you'll be making decisions that matter for your home.

Enjoy the process. Lean into it with the mind-set that this is the last time you'll have to do a whole-home declutter because you'll be setting up systems and rituals that guide your future decisions in subtle yet mindful ways. Better yet, you won't feel like you're doing a whole-home declutter because you'll be building in efficient systems and effective rituals that will prevent clutter from accumulating in the future and that you enjoy.

Seven Peaceful Home Guidelines

LIFE IS TOO SHORT TO SPEND IT CLEANING AND MAINTAINING STUFF. SO THESE seven guidelines can be a helpful place to start as you establish systems and rituals. If you're struggling to get motivated, think in terms of your "tomorrow self." Will your tomorrow self thank you for dealing with the clutter in the kitchen when she comes downstairs to a clean sink in the morning?

The following little steps will make things easier as you go.

- **Take it out; put it away.** Repeat this mantra out loud or in your head. Write it on a sticky note and teach it to your kids. It helps keep stuff from multiplying. After using something, put it away. This includes toys, papers, dishes, blankets—anything and everything. Take that extra step and probably an additional second or two to grab that book and bring it upstairs with you.

- **Deal with clutter daily.** It comes in every day, so deal with it every day to keep it from piling up. Set a timer for five minutes and deal with that stack of papers, incoming mail, the pile of stuff you keep moving from one place to the other. Repeat this daily, and you'll soon be in the habit of decluttering.

- **One in; one out.** While you're working through this book or just living your life, it might be helpful to let something go before you bring something new into the house. If you have a lot to let go of, you might need to establish a "one in, *two* out" practice so you're clearing out more than you're bringing in. Or perhaps you designate a "no spend" month or two (in which you buy only necessities) while you're working through this book.

- **Practice regular decluttering.** Follow my system for decluttering and set up four baskets/bins/bags for things you're going through: keep, toss, relocate, donate.

- **No more junk drawers.** A junk drawer is just that—full of junk waiting to be put where it belongs. Whether you have one junk drawer or ten, go through the contents and give each drawer a specific purpose.

- **Group like with like.** Think of a silverware drawer: forks go with forks, spoons go with spoons . . . and you know where everything belongs. Use this as a guiding principle as you set up your home systems.

- **Zones make everything run a little more smoothly.** The next step after "group like with like" is putting things in a zone. Zones can be anywhere in your home and are simply places where you put groups of things that you use for a specific purpose. For example, coffee mugs, coffee, and your coffeemaker all go together in your coffee zone.

You don't have to put all these guidelines in place right away—maybe choose one to start with and see what happens. I'll refer back to them and use them to help guide you as you establish systems and rituals in your home.

PART II

the clean home reset

CHAPTER 8

The Clean Home Reset Checklist

WE'RE GOING TO MOVE THROUGH YOUR HOME IN A SIMPLE WAY, AT YOUR PACE, adding systems and pairing them with rituals to achieve meaningful results. By the time you've completed the Clean Home Reset, you will feel lighter, more at ease, and ready for all these systems and rituals to do their thing. Use this book as a journal. Take your time, think through your decisions, and don't rush the process. You're making changes that will affect your home for the long term. This is the good stuff, the messy middle, and though it's going to be a little bit uncomfortable, I promise it will be so, so worth it!

I've divided this section of the book into areas of the home. I intentionally start with the room that has the biggest impact on daily life and will show the most beneficial and obvious results—the kitchen. As the heart of the home, the kitchen is essential to your success. I suggest proceeding in the order I lay out in the book rather than skipping around. This will help you address the biggest potential trouble spots first, so you'll get those big wins and move through the rest of your home with confidence. If you don't have one of the areas addressed in the book, skip over it to the next. Some areas will need more work than others, but you'll be setting up systems and rituals to create a calm home with just the right amount of order.

View this workbook as a love letter to your home. Mark it up, take notes, use the spaces provided to make a little check mark next to the systems and rituals you want to try. Read a bit, then try something. Read a little more, then try another idea. If something doesn't work, don't worry about it. This is all about finding what works for you, so you can always try something else! There's no pressure, no right or wrong, and no timeline. I'm rooting for you!

Following is a quick rundown of what we'll be resetting during our Clean Home Reset (see next page). Keep in mind that this should cover just about every area of your home, but if you have another area you'd like to cover, you'll see a spot where you can make a note and add it to the list. Use this as your master list as you proceed. Check off each area as you create systems and rituals and declutter.

Checklist

KITCHEN

○ storage + organization
○ food storage
○ meal planning
○ grocery shopping
○ food prep

BATHROOMS

○ storage + organization
○ paper products
○ towels + linens
○ toiletries + makeup
○ cleaning supplies
○ medicine + first aid

BEDROOMS

○ pillows
○ bed linens
○ bedside items

CLOTHING

○ hangers
○ hampers
○ out-of-season clothing
○ other family members' clothing

LINENS + LAUNDRY

○ laundry piles
○ laundry baskets + hampers
○ laundry supplies
○ laundry system
○ linen closet

LIVING SPACES

○ books + magazines
○ pillows + blankets
○ lighting
○ coffee table + surfaces

OFFICE + PAPERWORK

○ mail
○ bills
○ filing system
○ office supplies
○ photos and kids' artwork

ENTRYWAY + MUDROOM

○ shoes
○ coats
○ multi-use spaces
○ backpacks + bags

KIDS' ROOMS + SPACES

○ getting kids involved
○ toys + books

GARAGE

○ storage and organization

VEHICLES

○ Clutter and garbage
○ Cleaning supplies

CLEANING ROUTINE

○ daily
○ weekly
○ rotating

OTHER

○
○
○

CHAPTER 9

Kitchen:
Storage + Organization

LET'S START WITH A KITCHEN ASSESSMENT. WHAT ARE YOUR BIGGEST KITCHEN stressors? You know, the things that make you sigh when you realize that they've piled up *again* or that they're still where you left them? Maybe your new pantry organizer is sitting empty while what was supposed to go in it is sitting six inches from its proper home. Think of these stressors, whatever they are, as Pain Points that make daily life difficult. The process isn't working or you put off the completion of the task because you just don't like doing it.

In order to decide what systems and rituals to put into place in the kitchen, you need to determine *what* is causing you stress, disorder, or both. Once you understand the stressors, or Pain Points, you can determine the best possible solution, and that, my friend, is where you'll start to see the beauty in the way routines and rhythms fit together for a calm and stress-free home.

I'll go first—below are my Pain Points in the kitchen.

- Dishes on the counter and in the sink

- Loading and unloading the dishwasher

- Kitchen gadgets and small appliances cluttering the counter

- Mail on the counter

- Stuff on the kitchen table that doesn't belong there

- Crumbs under the kitchen table from a couple of meals ago

Write down a few of your own Pain Points—things that cause you stress or are bothersome in the kitchen.

_____

_____

_____

Do you have a system in place for doing any of the things that cause stress or even for those that are just an annoyance in the kitchen? What have you tried? What do you think might work? If the system you have in place isn't working, don't assume that it's not going to work _ever_: it might just need a little tweaking. There's nothing wrong with tweaking a system until it works—not everything works on the first try. If you've tried tweaking a system but haven't paired it with a ritual, try that before scrapping the system altogether.

Systems for the Kitchen

Much like any other Pain Point, this one involves things that get daily use but aren't put away regularly or don't have a home. I find that the best way to deal with this Pain Point is to take inventory of what I have, edit the inventory and keep only what I use, then put things away in strategic zones. I'll show you how below.

INVENTORY

Let's start by taking your dishes out of the cupboard or shelves. Yes, take them all out. Once you have everything pulled out, follow the Clean Mama declutter method. If there's anything that can be donated or that's broken or chipped, put those things in a donate or toss/recycle receptacle. Then sort and organize the dishes by type and stack them on a counter or table. Small plates, small bowls, large plates, large bowls, mugs, cups, glasses—all of it. Assess how many of each you have and determine if you have too many, not enough, or just the right amount. I recommend four to six complete place settings for one to three people and ten to twelve place settings for four to six people. If you have seven or more people in your family, you probably need sixteen place settings.

QUICK TIP

You might also want to edit your pots, pans, serving ware, and small appliances. Remember: it takes some time on the front end, but having an edited, organized kitchen will make things so much easier in the long run.

EDIT

Think about when and how you use your dishes and glasses. That will help you determine how much to keep out for daily use. Is someone home for all three meals a day? Or do you grab a cup of coffee and not come home until dinner? Maybe you've broken four glasses in the last couple of months and haven't replaced them, so one of your Pain Points is that you're always running out of glasses. Or maybe you've never used the last half a dozen plates in that stack—ever. Count up what you have, decide what you need for a day in the life of your home, and set the extras aside. This is something you'll want to assess based on your eating habits and needs. If you want to do a dry run to make sure you have enough, keep what you think you'll need and put the extras in a box out of the kitchen. Give it a week or so, then see if you need those extra place settings.

Make a note below of what you need.

_____

_____

_____

_____

REORGANIZE

Once you've gone through your current dish and glass situation and edited it down to just the right amount, consider where you store your dishes and glassware. Are they close to each other? Are they close to the sink and dishwasher? Then establish a zone—the dishes and glassware zone. You want to be able to stand at the sink and/or dishwasher and move no more than one to two steps to put those dishes and glasses away. This is efficiency at its finest.

When you're finished, put all the dishes, mugs, and glasses away into the cabinets or shelving space in the correct zone.

PAIN POINT: Cluttered Silverware and Utensil Drawers
SOLUTION: Drawer Organizers

INVENTORY AND EDIT

As you did with your dishes and glassware, quickly pull out your silverware and utensils. Take a few minutes to sort through any duplicates and extras. Keep what you use often: if you haven't used something in a month or so, it's probably not necessary. Make a note of anything that might be getting a little worn down, such as a spatula with a wobbly rubber head, and make a note to replace it on your next trip to Target.

QUICK TIP

Keep the kids from getting up from the table by using a tabletop cutlery organizer. Store napkins, silverware, and straws in the organizer, and no one needs to get up when a fork falls on the floor.

REORGANIZE

How do you have your silverware organized? I like a good divided drawer organizer and will look for one that matches the interior of the drawer. But you might want to look for one made of plastic, wire, wood, or even wicker. A drawer organizer also works well for kitchen utensils; alternatively, you can store frequently used utensils by the stove in a crock or vase.

If you're short on storage, a cutlery caddy is a great choice. You can use it to bring utensils from the sink or dishwasher back to the table at mealtimes. On the internet, you can even find custom drawer dividers sized to fit your drawers perfectly as well as a DIY method for making your own.

INVENTORY AND EDIT

Often we have way too many spices, and many of them are expired, taking up space in a cabinet or drawer. The rule of thumb is that you should only keep your spices for six months, though I often keep them for a full year. Spices don't really go "bad": they're not going to hurt you if you use them past their expiration date, but they won't have much flavor. Not sure if a spice is still spicy? Sprinkle a little in your hand and rub it between your fingers. If it smells fragrant or pungent, it's still fresh enough to use. If it doesn't have much of an aroma, or the color looks faded and old, give that spice jar a toss.

If it's a spice you bought for a certain recipe but have never used again, toss it. Next time you want to make that recipe, try buying a small amount of the spice in the bulk section of the supermarket—or borrow a tablespoon of it from a friend.

If you notice that you have a spice you only use in very small quantities but you bought a big jar of it at Costco, make a mental note. When you run out, buy a smaller container.

Create custom spice blends for spices you typically use combination, such as a Mexican blend of paprika, cumin, chili powder, oregano, and garlic powder or an Italian blend of oregano, basil, marjoram, rosemary, and thyme. Spoon equal amounts of each spice into a small canning jar, or adjust the quantities to taste, then blend with a table knife. Write the name on the top or side of the jar with an oil-based pen.

First decide where to keep your spices. Some people like to use a drawer; some people prefer a cabinet. Storing spices by the stove keeps them within the cooking zone, so you won't have to take more than a couple of steps when you need a dash of salt or cinnamon.

Now create storage a system. This will take a little effort, but once it's in place, you'll never think about it again! I store my spices on tiered acrylic racks so I can easily see what I have. I also keep baking ingredients on the shelf above the spices on a turntable—chocolate chips, honey, powdered sugar, cocoa powder, molasses, and so on. I use another turntable for cooking ingredients such as oils, vinegars, and a large container of salt. Not only does this keep drips and spills confined to the turntable, making it super easy to wipe clean, it also makes the ingredients easy to access. If you don't have space for turntables, consider using a handled basket or bin instead.

If you only use a few spices when you cook, adopt a minimalist approach: buy small quantities in bulk and put them in small glass jars. Alternatively, if you're really into cooking and baking, create your own spice blends and jar them up and label them.

When you bring new spices in, use an oil-based pen to mark the bottom of the jars with the date you purchased them so you can just turn the jar over the next time you're trying to remember how old a spice really is.

PAIN POINT: Inefficient Kitchen Set Up
SOLUTION: Set Up Zones

As I mentioned above, creating zones in your kitchen will ease headaches you might not realize you had. Following are the most important zones to set up.

DISHWARE ZONE

(See page 63.)

KITCHEN TOWELS ZONE

Keep kitchen towels close to the dishware zone to make it easy to grab one when you want to dry your hands. I also find that storing dish towels and bar mop towels (the kind made of terry cloth) near the sink makes it just a little bit easier to get in the habit of putting out fresh towels daily. I keep a large glass jar on the counter next to the sink stuffed with rolled-up bar mop towels in lieu of paper towels.

COOKING ZONE

- **Spice rack or drawer.** Storing herbs and spices in the area where you use them most limits your steps in the kitchen and ups your efficiency when it comes to cooking and baking.

- **Daily use items.** Keep those ingredients that you use daily or almost daily on the counter if you have the space for them. I keep salt, pepper, olive oil, garlic, and small utensils in a jar on a pretty wooden cutting board to the left of the stove so I can move the board and clean under it easily. If you don't have enough counter space, you could put these items in a bin or basket and store the basket in a cupboard or the pantry. That way you can just take out the basket before you get ready to cook instead of reaching for each item individually.

- **Measuring cups and spoons.** Create a mini zone within reach of your herbs and spices—and within reach of your stove—where you can store your measuring cups and spoons. A mini zone will help you be more efficient while cooking and baking, and it will keep those frequently used items within reach.

- **Knife block or drawer.** Having a safe and handy space for kitchen knives will make it easy to grab one when you need it or to change your knife choice as you're cooking. A knife block, magnet, or drawer are all great choices. The main idea is to have your knives easily accessible to adults but not to children. Take it a step further and place your knives by your cutting boards so you can grab both at the same time for quick chopping and prepping.

REFRIGERATOR AND FREEZER ZONE

If you struggle with refrigerator and freezer disorganization, you probably need to establish zones within each appliance. This can be done simply by cleaning out the refrigerator or freezer, organizing the food by category, then returning it to its proper zone. You can write the name of each zone on the bins or door using a dry erase marker (just wet a cloth and wipe clean whenever you reorganize).

Having designated zones in your refrigerator and freezer makes it easy to see what you have at a glance and keeps things organized. Establish zones for fruit, vegetables, beverages, things you use in meals that are on-deck for that night or the next, deli items (such as cheese and cold cuts), and condiments. I separate condiments vertically— sweet things (such as jam and maple syrup) go on the bottom and savory things (such as salad dressings, ketchup, and mustard) go on the top. If you have a refrigerator with two doors, you can split the condiments up by left and right doors. For snacks, I keep a protein bin in the refrigerator so any of us can quickly grab an easy-to-eat protein-rich snack. We keep yogurt, string cheese, and hard-boiled eggs in this bin. I would rather have the kids reach for a protein-rich snack instead of crackers or chips.

- **Next to the sink.** Alongside the sink and dishwasher, keep hand soap, dish soap, counter spray, cleaning cloths, and dishwasher pods or soap. Put your hand soap, dish soap, and counter spray on a small tray for easy cleaning—just move the tray and clean underneath it. Keep sponges and scrub brushes accessible and out in the open to help them dry out quickly. I like to put them brush side up in a cute container.

- **Under the sink.** Store items that you need for cleaning under the sink—I keep extra dishwasher pods, ingredients for my Stone-Cleaning Spray, hydrogen peroxide in a spray bottle for disinfection, my Nightly Sink Scrub, and a container where I can toss hand towels and bar mop towels that need to be laundered. I use a turntable under the sink for easy access to under-the-sink items.

- **Cabinet door.** Put a removable hook inside the door to the cabinet under your kitchen sink where you can hang damp (not wet) dishcloths so they dry thoroughly and don't get smelly.

PAIN POINT: Cleaning the Kitchen Each Night Is a Tiring Process
SOLUTION: Clean Smarter, Not Harder

CLEAN AS YOU GO

It sounds easy, but we all know it takes a little (or a lot of) effort to do this. If you're in the kitchen cooking, keep a damp bar mop towel near you to wipe up little drips and spills. If you're waiting for something on the stove, use this time to wipe counters and hand-wash dishes and cookware. You can also use cooking time to wipe cabinet fronts and the fronts of appliances.

SOAK POTS AND PANS

As you're cooking, put dirty pots and pans in the sink to soak. This makes it easier to clean up and gives you a head start on the dishes. The bonus? No stuck-on food.

START RIGHT AWAY

Don't go sit down in front of the TV after dinner. Take the time right away to clean up the kitchen. Cleanup is easier all around when you take care of it right away. Load the dishwasher, wipe the counters, and make this a habit.

PUT SILVERWARE IN A COLANDER IN THE SINK

Keep that silverware together and prevent it from inadvertently heading down the drain or disposal by gathering all the silverware and placing it in a colander or bowl in the sink. Fill the bowl with hot water if the utensils need a little soak or rinse them and let the water drain out of the colander.

STACK PLATES BEFORE YOU WASH OR RINSE THEM

Stack plates and bowls on the counter as you're clearing the table and rinse them in the sink before putting them in the dishwasher. This minimizes effort and makes this process go a little bit quicker.

PUT YOUR SPONGE OR SCRUB BRUSH IN THE DISHWASHER

Run your sponge or scrub brush through the dishwasher nightly. Germs can be spread by a dirty sponge or scrub brush, so take that extra second and put it in the dishwasher or sanitize it in the microwave before you leave the kitchen.

RUN THE DISHWASHER BEFORE BED

Once the kitchen is cleaned and the dishes are loaded, the final step is to run the dishwasher. Look at those clear and clean counters and listen to that whirring dishwasher! Oddly enough, that small satisfaction can give you a good feeling at the end of a long day.

PAIN POINT: Waking Up to Dishes Still in the Sink

SOLUTION: Nightly Kitchen Reset

One task that my family has successfully made into a routine is a nightly kitchen reset. We do this together as a family, which is really helpful and makes this somewhat daunting task quite a bit easier. Keeping up with it nightly is a surefire way to keep the kitchen clean all or most of the time. It's also a gift to yourself when you wake up in the morning. A clean kitchen is much more enjoyable to cook in as well.

Furthermore, keeping your kitchen clean helps prevent food-borne illnesses. The kitchen sink is one of the dirtiest and germiest places in the house. Cleaning it nightly is important. Taking just five to ten minutes nightly to clean it pays off many times over each and every day.

Following a system for this gives everyone a job and a game plan. Below is what it looks like at my house.

- Clear the table—everyone brings his or her own dishes to the counter

- Rinse dishes—in my house, this is my husband's job

- Load the dishwasher—this is my job

- Hand-wash dishes that can't go in the dishwasher

- Wipe the counters and the kitchen table

- Wipe the stovetop if necessary—I usually do this while I'm cooking just to keep the mess at a minimum

- Scrub the sink with my Nightly Sink Scrub (see page 78)

- Check the floor—sweep or vacuum if necessary

- Make sure the coffeepot is clean and ready for the next day

- Put out fresh hand towels and bar mop or dish towels

- Run the dishwasher

Looking for ways to get the family involved? Assign specific jobs to everyone. This can be done on the fly each evening, or if everyone likes having a specific job, let them do what they like to do. You can also rotate jobs weekly. Some ideas for after-dinner jobs include stacking plates and bringing them to the counter, gathering silverware in a colander, rinsing dishes, putting dishes in the dishwasher, putting glassware in the dishwasher, hand-washing dishes, drying dishes, wiping the kitchen table, wiping the counters, and scrubbing the sink.

You can also put on some music, a podcast, or an audiobook to make it more fun to clean the kitchen together.

Write down the tasks you need to complete for a nightly kitchen reset at your house.

Think of ways you can delegate tasks to family members to get this done quickly.

_____

_____

_____

_____

PAIN POINT: My Kids Don't Know How to Help in the Kitchen
SOLUTION: Kid Drawer

If you have young kids who use their own plates, utensils, and cups, put the kid-safe dishes in an accessible drawer. Even kids as young as two or three can get on board with this, making it easy for them to get a bowl, cup, and spoon and set their own spots at the table or grab the utensils and dishes and bring them to you at the stove. Not only does this teach independence, it also frees up space in your cupboards—your dishes will fit better and look more aesthetically pleasing (sorry, kiddos). If you don't have a drawer to spare, you can stack and stash the kid stuff easily in a bin or basket.

Rituals for the Kitchen

All right, so we've started putting some new systems in place. These systems will help your kitchen run more smoothly and efficiently as well as reduce your workload. But remember, when you pair a system with a ritual—something that brings you peace—that's where the magic happens. These are our Happy Tasks!

Is there anything you feel is already operating as a Happy Task in your kitchen? Are there things you enjoy (or at east don't mind) doing when you're there? Write them down in the space provided.

Here are a few rituals that make me feel calmer in the kitchen.

MORNING

Empty the Dishwasher While the Coffee or Tea Brews

Pair emptying the dishwasher with getting your morning drink going: coffee, tea, lemon water, smoothie—whatever it is, pairing the thing you look forward to with something you don't will help you get both accomplished quickly.

MIDDAY

Clean Up the Kitchen After Every Lunch

I know this doesn't sound like something that will bring you joy, but if you're continually stressed out because it seems like there's always a mountain of dishes to do, this might really help. Especially if you're a dish procrastinator, it might be helpful for you to do a quick cleanup after every meal. Clearing after lunch gets the kitchen ready to go for dinner so you're not frantically washing dishes before you can cook the evening meal. Getting

QUICK TIP

When unloading the dishwasher, it's easiest to stack the plates, bowls, and other dishes on the counter and then put them away all at once instead of putting them away one by one. If you're washing and drying the dishes by hand, apply this same principle: put a towel on the counter and stack them up as you dry.

into this habit will make cleaning up easier because you're doing it multiple times during the day versus all at once over the course of a day or two, and you can enlist the help of family members.

Read a Book or Do a Crossword Puzzle

If you have time for a midday break, take a few minutes to bask in your clean, peaceful kitchen by sitting at the table with a book, a crossword puzzle, and maybe a fizzy beverage. Our homes are meant for us to enjoy!

EVENING

These work well when paired with cleaning up the kitchen after dinner, or as part of the kitchen reset.

Wipe the Counters and Table After Dinner

Again, I know that doing more cleaning doesn't sound like a pleasurable activity. What *is* pleasurable is the peace of mind that comes from doing a simple five-minute task that brings quick results. We've discussed before how visual clutter can lead to making us feel anxious and stressed, so seeing clean, uncluttered counters will be a relief and one less thing to think about. It's simple: when mealtime is over, wipe down the counters and the table (or ask a family member to do so). It's not always the easiest thing to do, especially at the end of the day, but get in the habit of doing it by telling yourself that you'll appreciate it tomorrow. Do this a couple of times, and you'll see the benefit and start to look forward to it.

Make Hand-Washing Dishes Pleasurable

That's right! Hand-washing dishes doesn't have to be such a chore. Put your hand soap, dish soap, and counter spray on a tray or pretty dish. Place these items next to the sink for easy access. Use products and tools that you enjoy—perhaps those with a calming scent—as well as dishwashing gloves that keep your hands soft. Get a gel mat to stand on so it's easier on your back. And don't forget to turn on some music!

Put Out Fresh Hand Towels and Dish Towels After Evening Cleaning

Not only is putting out fresh towels a hygienic ritual, it's also nice to dry your hands on a towel you know is clean. If you use pretty hand towels, it's a little more enjoyable. This finishing touch will take just a moment to do, but it's a simple little thing that pays big dividends.

Use My Nightly Sink Scrub

My favorite DIY recipe is also my favorite evening ritual—the Nightly Sink Scrub. This little recipe will change your evening kitchen routine forever. The best thing? It works on any sink type! Porcelain, stainless steel, acrylic, copper, stone—scrub away!

Every night after I put the dishes in the dishwasher and wipe the counters, I sprinkle a little of this mixture in the sink, add a squirt or two of dish soap or castile soap, and give the sink a good scrub. Rinse, then dry with a towel or just let it air dry. Put out a clean hand towel and walk away from the kitchen knowing it's reset for the next day.

The great thing about this recipe is that it's so simple to whip up. Not only does it smell good, it also does a great job of cleaning. You'll love it!

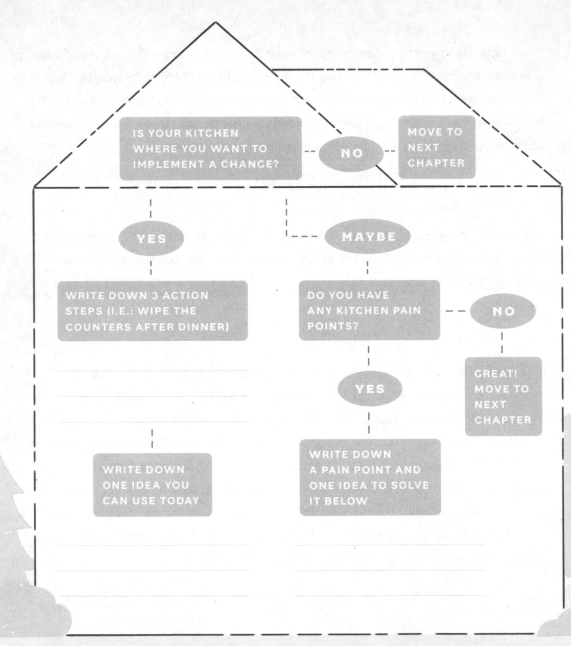

NIGHTLY SINK SCRUB

After the dishes are done for the night, sprinkle a bit of this in your sink and give it a little scrub. It will leave the surface sparkling clean.

INGREDIENTS

2 cups baking soda

20 drops essential oils—
I use 10 drops lemon and
10 drops clove

1 to 2 squirts liquid castile
soap or dish soap

SPECIAL EQUIPMENT

Container with a lid or
shaker top

Sink-safe scrub brush
or sponge

Pour the baking soda into your container. (I like using a mason jar.) Drop the essential oils on top of the baking soda and stir with a table knife to combine.

Wet your sink and sprinkle the scrub liberally over the surface. Squirt with castile soap or dish soap and scrub with the scrub brush or sponge. Rinse thoroughly and admire your clean and shiny sink.

Store the baking soda mixture under the sink; it will keep for several months.

Put a Simmer on the Stove

I love to make simmers. If you're feeling like you need a little pick-me-up or want to make your time in the kitchen more pleasant, try a simmer. I like to customize a couple of scents for each season with what I have on hand or am in the mood for. Mix one up and simmer it away on your stove or in a small slow cooker while you clean, and your mood will elevate in no time.

SIMMERS

Gather any combination of the following ingredients—you only need one, but I recommend two or three. My favorite is lemon and/or orange slices together with fresh rosemary leaves and vanilla extract.

INGREDIENTS

3 to 4 slices fresh citrus fruit, such as lemons, oranges, and/or limes

3 to 4 slices fresh apple

1 handful fresh cranberries

3 to 4 cardamom pods

2 to 3 cinnamon sticks

8 to 10 whole cloves

1 tablespoon fresh herbs

1 handful pine needles

2–3 drops vanilla, almond, or maple extract

1–2 drops essential oil of your choice

4 cups water

Combine your choice of aromatics with water in a medium saucepan and set over high heat. Bring to a boil, then reduce heat to low and maintain the mixture at a slow simmer for as long as you're in the kitchen. Add more water as needed.

CHAPTER 10

Kitchen: Meal Planning, Grocery Shopping, and Prep

MEAL PLANNING, GROCERY SHOPPING, AND PREP ARE LEARNED BEHAVIORS; I honestly don't think anyone is naturally gifted in all three areas at the same time. That said, I do think these skills are easily learned, hacked, and built upon. If you think you're hopeless and can't plan a menu to save your life, for example, I want to suggest some systems that can help.

When you plan your menu and your grocery-shopping runs, you'll find that you're in control of what you bring into the house, and you'll see that organizing your menu and trips to the store also allows you to organize your kitchen. When you have menus planned, there's generally a ripple effect—you'll eat better, spend less money, waste less food, and feel better about dinnertime.

I'll go first: following are my Pain Points when it comes to meal planning, grocery shopping, and prep:

- Forgetting my reusable bags

- Realizing that there isn't food in the fridge when it's too late (someone's hungry or it's dinnertime)

- Not buying enough food for the number of humans in the house

- Food waste—I hate remembering that I bought cucumbers only to find them slimy in the crisper

- Putting groceries away

- School lunches—they seem very time-consuming and labor-intensive for something so simple

Write down a few of your own Pain Point Tasks below—things that cause you stress or are bothersome when it comes to meal planning, meal prep, and grocery shopping.

Systems for Meal Planning, Grocery Shopping, and Prep

If you've never really put together a system for meal planning, grocery shopping, and prep, I suggest moving through the following systems in order. If you have a meal-planning system in place but need some ideas for tweaking it so that it works better, find tips in the upcoming sections that discuss weekly and monthly menus (see p. 84).

ASSESS HOW YOUR FAMILY EATS

Before we get into the nuts and bolts of meal planning, it helps to understand your family's specific needs. How many meals a week do you usually cook? Are there foods that are off-limits in your family because of dietary restrictions, allergies, or preferences? Maybe you can only cook at home three nights a week. If so, let's figure out how to stretch the meals you make so they'll last for seven days. Does your family like a full meal every night? Or is everyone okay with a leftovers bash once a week?

Also, think about what kind of meal planner you are. Do you like using cookbooks? A specific menu-planning website? A recipe binder? An internet search? Or do you cook without a recipe? Gather the reference materials you need, if any, and put them in a spot in your kitchen or wherever you do your menu planning. Jot down some thoughts about your meal planning process below.

USE A NOTEBOOK OR PLANNER FOR TRACKING MEALS

Writing down your proposed menu for the week is really helpful: you can refer to it as the week goes on, and you can return to it if you want to repeat a good week in the future. There are so many different methods to choose from: a chalkboard or whiteboard in the kitchen, where everyone can see what's for dinner; a paper notebook; a magnetized notepad on the fridge; an app that pulls up your menu for you. The object is to figure out a system that works for you, then implement it.

Writing down your menu also means you're not starting from scratch every week. Look back on past weeks and change only those things that need changing. Things you eat every week can remain on the plan. Remind yourself of meals your family loved, then slot one or two into the current week. This helps meal planning go much quicker!

If you haven't tried menu planning, you're missing out on a big productivity hack. But I get it: meal planning takes time, and if your family doesn't always want to eat what you want to cook, or if dinnertime is different for each member of the family, this is difficult. I'm going to suggest that you try it—even if just for a week. Make a list of your family's ten favorite simple meals below.

_____   _____

_____   _____

_____   _____

_____   _____

Now choose three of those meals and make a shopping list for their ingredients. Double the recipes so you can eat them for two nights instead of the usual one night.

For example, let's say the meals below are your family's favorites.

- Spaghetti with meat sauce

- Burrito bowls with chicken

- Turkey meatloaf with salad

If you double those recipes, you have six nights of dinners instead of just two, so you'll cook once and eat twice three times. I don't do this weekly, but I definitely do this at least one week per month. You can also repurpose the protein in each recipe. For example, you can use the chicken from the burrito bowls in a Mexican salad two nights later. See how it feels for one week, and see if you can repeat the plan the following week. If you can do this two weeks in a row, you're on a roll!

Menu Plan Brainstorming

MONDAY IDEAS

TUESDAY IDEAS

WEDNESDAY IDEAS

THURSDAY IDEAS

FRIDAY IDEAS

Prefer a more traditional approach? Plug your favorites into your calendar or planner, make your list, and head to the grocery store. Alternatively, plan "theme" nights: for example, Meatless Monday, Taco Tuesday, Kids' Choice Wednesday, Chicken Dinner Thursday, Pizza Night Friday, Steak Saturday, Extended Family Dinner Sunday.

The decision-making process is what can complicate and derail your meal planning, but when you simplify your decisions, you make planning easier. Set yourself up for success by making it as simple as you can, and you'll be able to gain momentum. Once you find some success, you'll see the benefit and be encouraged to continue making those menu plans and getting those dinners on the table. You'll be surprised how it changes dinnertime.

CHOOSE A DAY OF THE WEEK TO GROCERY SHOP

I like to grocery shop on Fridays. The stores are fully stocked, the food is fresh, and I can typically avoid the weekend rush. When I was working outside the home I would stop by on my way home from work on Friday and grab a rotisserie chicken as well as food for the weekend and the beginning of the coming week. We'd eat the chicken with a salad for dinner and have a fridge full of food so there was no need to head out to the store when everyone else was shopping. Maybe you like shopping on Tuesdays or on Sunday afternoon. But if you have a specific day for it, you'll find that you're more likely to successfully plan meals and that your shopping proceeds more efficiently. If you feel like planning meals and grocery shopping is too much to do on the same day, split it up so it's an easier task.

You can also use a grocery pickup or delivery service to cut the trip to the supermarket short or eliminate it altogether. If you feel overwhelmed with shopping or are making frequent trips to the store, try automating your supply runs this way. It's a real time saver and can be helpful in a pinch.

SHOP WITH A LIST

I make a shopping list while I do my meal planning on Fridays—I'm much more success-ful (and spend less money!) when I go prepared with a list and shop from it. I also keep a running list of things we're almost out of at home. I organize the list by type of store—online and brick-and-mortar. I add the grocery items to my brick-and-mortar list and when there are enough items to warrant an order from an online shop, I place my order. This helps me keep tabs on food inventory and ensures that I'm not forgetting something at the store.

MANAGE FOOD INVENTORY REGULARLY

Keep a list of the foods you have in storage if you find that you're losing track of what you have. How many times do you pick up a jar of tomato sauce at the store only to get home and find you already have three of them in your pantry? By keeping a list—on a white-board, a magnetized pad on the fridge, an app, or a meal-planning notebook—you can remember what you have in the pantry, refrigerator, and/or freezer and avoid overbuying and food waste.

TREAT YOUR FOOD STORAGE AS A SUPERMARKET WOULD: FIRST IN, FIRST OUT

When you come back from grocery shopping, take an extra second or two and pull out the old items from the refrigerator. Then place the new items in and put the old items in front of them. This first in, first out method keeps you from finding expired food at the back of the refrigerator.

Category Grocery Shopping List

FRUIT	VEGGIES	MEATS	DELI
○	○	○	○
○	○	○	○
○	○	○	○

DAIRY	BEVERAGES	BAKERY/BREADS	FROZEN FOODS
○	○	○	○
○	○	○	○
○	○	○	○

CANNED GOODS	RICE/ PASTA	CEREAL/ GRAINS	BAKING/SPICES
○	○	○	○
○	○	○	○
○	○	○	○

CONDIMENTS	SPECIALTY	HOUSEHOLD	TOILETRIES
○	○	○	○
○	○	○	○
○	○	○	○

PAPER GOODS	BABIES/KIDS	PETS	OTHER
○	○	○	○
○	○	○	○
○	○	○	○

ESTABLISH A SYSTEM FOR GROCERIES COMING IN

Next, unload your shopping bags. Use the countertop or kitchen table as your work surface. Put away frozen and perishable foods first. Put produce on the counter by the kitchen sink (you'll take care of it when you do your food prep), then put away the canned goods, bread, and snacks. Once that's done, spray and wipe down the area you placed the items on with a disinfecting spray to kill any germs you might have brought in from the store.

Designate a Space for Extras

If you've ever worked at a restaurant, in retail, or in a grocery store, you're probably familiar with the term "backstock." Backstock is simply extra inventory, or overstock: things you know you'll need soon but don't need to display right now. We have two shallow pull-out rolling baskets in our pantry for just that—backstock. If you shop at a warehouse club, you'll find this especially helpful. Use your backstock in a way that makes sense, but I encourage you not to buy too much. Overstock will turn into clutter and soon feel stressful.

PREP FRUITS AND VEGETABLES
AS SOON AS YOU GET HOME

After you've put your other groceries away, wash, cut, and prep any produce you'll be using during the next couple of days so it will be accessible and ready. If there are items you won't be using within a day or two, put them in the fridge or on the counter and wash as needed. You'll find that you eat better when healthful foods are already washed and ready to bite into. Preparing your produce in advance also saves time because you aren't pulling a cucumber out to wash and cut every day for your salad. You'll feel so much happier when your meals come together more quickly.

PUT YOUR MEAT ON A SHEET PAN IN THE REFRIGERATOR

I keep a quarter sheet pan in the refrigerator where I put packages of meat. If something is thawing, it goes there; if it's just waiting a day or two to be cooked, it hangs out on the tray. This keeps any meat juices contained and allows me to see at a glance what I have ready for cooking.

AND A RELATED BONUS: CHANGE WHEN AND HOW YOU MAKE SCHOOL LUNCHES

In my house, the kids are old enough to mostly make their own lunches, but I'm still in the kitchen overseeing the process. I make sure we always have lunch components on hand so they can grab those items and put their own lunches together. Our components? A grain (muffin, sandwich, or crackers), two fruits or vegetables, a protein snack (usually cheese or yogurt), and a water bottle. Each kid likes different things, but this helps them make healthful food choices and learn to be responsible for their meals. If your mornings feel crowded, work on lunches as you're cleaning up the kitchen in the evening. Kids can still take charge of this task, and you'll still be in the kitchen keeping an eye on the choices. Put anything that needs refrigeration in the refrigerator overnight, then toss it in the lunch bag before or after breakfast the next day.

Rituals for Meal Planning, Grocery Shopping, and Prep

Now that we've got some great systems to put into place, let's add in some rituals. These tasks are similar to systems and will help you enjoy the fruits of your meal-prep labor!

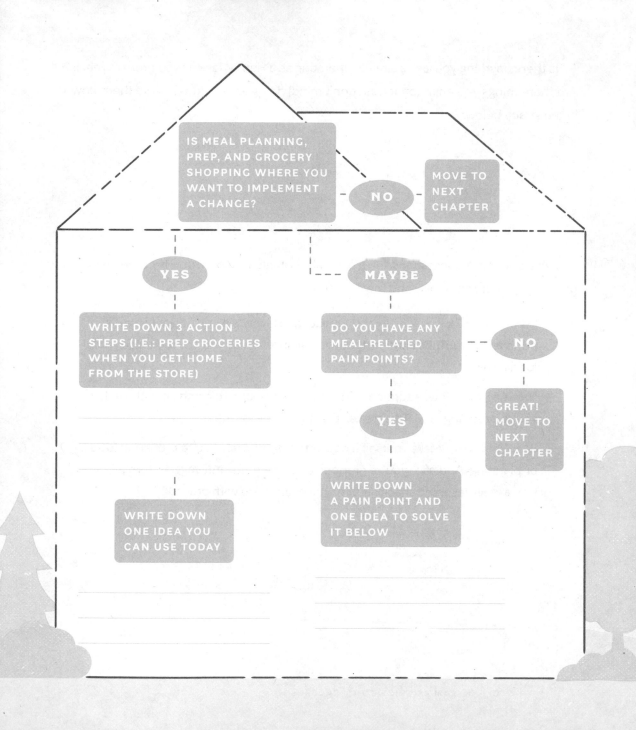

IS MEAL PLANNING, PREP, AND GROCERY SHOPPING WHERE YOU WANT TO IMPLEMENT A CHANGE?

NO

MOVE TO NEXT CHAPTER

YES

MAYBE

WRITE DOWN 3 ACTION STEPS (I.E.: PREP GROCERIES WHEN YOU GET HOME FROM THE STORE)

DO YOU HAVE ANY MEAL-RELATED PAIN POINTS?

NO

YES

GREAT! MOVE TO NEXT CHAPTER

WRITE DOWN ONE IDEA YOU CAN USE TODAY

WRITE DOWN A PAIN POINT AND ONE IDEA TO SOLVE IT BELOW

Is there anything you feel is already operating as a Happy Task as you prepare meals? Are there things you enjoy (or at least don't mind) doing as you cook? Write them down in the space below.

_____

_____

_____

Here are some suggestions for pleasurable rituals I enjoy when it comes to meal planning, grocery shopping, and meal prep.

- **Listen to music or a podcast.** Queue up a favorite album, Spotify playlist, podcast, or YouTube channel that you can listen to as you shop, chop, or put food away.

- **Call a friend.** Put headphones in, and call someone to catch up with while you're prepping food. This makes the time fly by for me.

- **Enjoy a snack.** Make yourself a cup of tea to sip while you're preparing food or planning. And after you've prepped all those fruits and veggies, turn a few into a well-deserved snack (and maybe even share with others!).

CHAPTER 11

Bathrooms

THE ROOM THAT WINS THE HARDEST TO CLEAN AND KEEP CLEAN AWARD? THE bathroom. Because it has a variety of surfaces, including tile, porcelain, and metal, and because it's almost always filled with moisture and frequently lacks adequate ventilation, it can be very difficult to clean. And let's face it: no one likes to clean the bathroom. But put a little time and thought into creating systems for the task, and you'll go a long way toward making cleaning—and using—the bathroom more enjoyable.

What are your biggest bathroom stressors? Is there a lingering odor? Always running out of toilet paper? No one putting the toilet paper back on the holder? Does it feel like it's so dirty that it would take you too long to clean?

In order to decide what systems and rituals to put into place in the bathroom, you need to determine *what* is causing you stress and why you aren't loving the bathroom. Once we get to the bottom of that, we'll fine-tune our tasks for success.

I'll go first—following are my Pain Points in the bathroom.

- Running out of toilet paper

- Kids leaving wet towels on the bathroom floor

- Not having clean towels

- Toiletries and other clutter on the counter

- Dirt on the counter

- Soap scum in the tub and shower

- Hard-water stains in the toilet

Write down a few Pain Points of your own—things that cause you stress or are bothersome in the bathroom.

_____

_____

_____

Do you have more than one bathroom? Use the space below to detail Pain Points in each one.

_____

_____

_____

Do you have a system already in place for any of the things that cause stress or are even just an annoyance in the bathroom? What have you tried? What do you think might work? As we did in the kitchen, let's see if we can tweak any of your systems to make them work better.

Systems for the Bathroom

PAIN POINT: Keeping Toiletries Organized
SOLUTION: Contain and Categorize

INVENTORY AND EDIT

Does your shower have empty or nearly empty bottles of shampoo sitting in it? Do you have loads of sample-size toiletries in your medicine cabinet? Below are a few ideas for getting your toiletries organized in minutes.

- Completely empty whatever space—drawer, shower stall, shower organizer, cabinet, counter—you're using to store your toiletries.

- Spray the area with your favorite all-purpose cleaner and wipe clean.

- Toss any containers that are empty or almost empty. Throw away items that you haven't used in the last month or don't see yourself using in the near future.

- Follow the first rule of organizing: group like items together. Put sample-size toiletries in a box, bin, or basket for guests or for future travel.

- Drawer dividers are your friends. If you don't have them in your bathroom drawers, consider installing them so your toiletries can stay organized. I use clear acrylic drawer organizers in every bathroom—measure and find ones that fit. They are amazing tools!

REORGANIZE

I use bins to store our personal-care products and toiletries in the bathroom cabinets. Everything falls into one of the following categories.

- Teeth and mouth

- Sun and travel

- Ear, nose, and throat

- Mani-pedi

- First aid

- Kid remedies

I like using open bins with handles because the handles make the bins easy to grab and because everything is exposed so you can easily see what you have. If the kids need a bandage, they know they'll find it in the first aid bin.

I also love placing my makeup and tools on a tray in the bathroom. It makes cleaning super easy: when I go to wipe down the counter, I simply put the tray on the floor, spray the counter with cleaner, and wipe.

Finally, look at your counters and decide what really must be there. Do you need to keep all those things on display? Determine what the necessities are and stash the non-dailies under the sink in storage containers or on turntables.

PAIN POINT: Limited Storage Space
SOLUTION: Smarter Storage

Not a lot of space? A good place to start is by condensing your toiletries down as much as you can—it'll simplify your routine and maximize the space you do have.

If you struggle to keep products contained under the bathroom sink, store them either in a container that you can pull out or in a divided lazy Susan. This keeps everything out of the way but still accessible.

Another good rule of thumb is to group like items together. Contact lens or glasses wearer? Take the lenses out of the packages and put them in a compartmentalized tray with your glasses case and glasses cleaner. Keep tooth-care products together in a drawer. Dedicate a drawer to hair-care items such as brushes, combs, and styling aids. When you put like items together, you aren't spending time searching for them.

Finally—and this is a funny thing to talk about, but it's a good example of something that doesn't matter until it does—if you don't have adequate toilet paper storage, put several rolls in something decorative like a basket or toilet paper holder next to the toilet. Trust me, it will make a difference when it matters most. If you do have cabinets near your toilets, stock them with toilet paper and clean towels.

PAIN POINT: Bathrooms Are No Fun to Clean
SOLUTION: Bathroom Speed-Cleaning Routine

Speed cleaning bathrooms is my favorite method to get in and get out as quickly as possible while ensuring a sanitary space. If this looks familiar to Monday: Bathroom Cleaning Day in chapter 5, it's because I want you to experience bathroom bliss, and I know that this is a huge Pain Point for so many readers.

- **Mirrors.** Spray a microfiber cloth with glass cleaner and wipe the mirror clean. The microfiber keeps the surface lint-free and streak-free. Reuse the cloth in each bathroom.

- **Sink, toilet surfaces, tub, and shower.** Next, quickly spray these with disinfecting cleaner and leave undisturbed. (If you don't use a tub or shower regularly, you don't need to clean it weekly.) I use nontoxic disinfecting cleaners. They work just as well as other cleaners and aren't harmful to you or your family.

- **Toilet bowl.** Sprinkle or squirt your preferred cleaner into the toilet bowl, brush, then flush.

- **The wipe-down.** Thoroughly wipe the sink, toilet, and the tub or shower. Remember, they've already been sprayed, so you're just wiping. Take care to use a separate cloth or microfiber towel for each task—the sink, toilet, bathtub, and shower—to avoid cross-contamination. Don't forget the base of the toilets. I wipe these last.

- **Repeat.** Repeat the above four steps in each bathroom in your home. Once you've finished, place the dirty cleaning cloths in a container for laundering.

- **Replace towels.** To finish, put out fresh hand and bath towels to give your bathroom that "just cleaned" touch.

BATHROOM CLEANING CADDY

I have kept a bathroom cleaning caddy under my bathroom sink for years. This has really helped me, because I find that having a few quick cleaning supplies at the ready for any little mess that might occur—or for Mondays, when I clean the bathrooms—is a real time saver.

If you'd like to put together your own caddy, all you need to do is find a bucket or a caddy that has a handle so you can tote it around the bathroom as you clean or carry it to your other bathrooms when you're finished with the first one. Then gather your supplies. Think about what supplies you use most and put them together in your caddy. See page 40 for a list of suggestions.

INVENTORY AND EDIT

Every bathroom most likely needs a different system for towels. Start by assessing your towel situation. Gather your towels from each bathroom, and put the matching towels together. For example, my husband and I use only white bath towels, but the kids have patterned towels, and sometimes they get mixed up with ours and vice versa. Once you get your complete sets together, if there are tattered towels or towels that need to be replaced, toss them. I keep old towels on hand for dog baths and times when the kids are sick and need a path around their beds or to the bathroom to minimize accidents, but you can also donate old towels to your local animal shelter or veterinarian.

REORGANIZE

Decide how you want to fold your towels—in half, in thirds, or another way. This ensures that everything fits neatly and can be located easily in your linen closet. Fold the towels and put them away, then the next time you launder them, fold them the same way before you put them in the closet or in the bathroom.

If you find that you're gathering lots of bath towels on the floor or that it's hard for family members to hang them on the towel bars after they've used them, put a small basket on the bathroom floor. Put it right around the area where the towels usually end up, and I bet they might find their way to the basket rather than the floor. Once it's full, toss the towels in the wash or put them in the hamper for Saturday—Sheets + Towels Day.

Rituals for Bathrooms

Is there anything you feel is already operating as a Happy Task in the bathroom? Are there things you enjoy (or at least don't mind) doing when you're in there? Write them down in the space below.

QUICK TIP

For kids who throw towels on the floor, place a hook or towel bar at their own height right above or near where their towels usually land. Ask them to hang up their towels after every shower or bath until they finally start to comply. Consistency will win this battle.

PUT FACIAL WASHCLOTHS ON THE COUNTER

This ritual is inexpensive but feels luxurious. First I buy a couple of packages of thin white washcloths—they're usually packaged as a set. You could also buy colored cloths, but the important part is that they shouldn't have any trim on them. They're just sewn around the edges and are very thin. Then I put them in a small wire basket and keep it on the counter by the bathroom sink. Every night I use a cloth to take my makeup off and wash my face. Not only do they dry quickly, they also wash up beautifully. No more makeup on your good washcloths.

I rinse them thoroughly after I use them, and this takes care of most of the makeup. Then I put them in the hamper and wash them in hot water in the machine, right along with our white bath towels, using laundry soap, white vinegar, and an oxygen whitener. Then I dry them in the dryer as usual.

I find these washcloths last a few years. I've purchased them just three times, and then only when the ones I had were dingy and needed to be replaced. They make good rags if you want to recycle them for another use, too.

USE WHITE TOWELS FOR A SPA-LIKE FEEL

I used to be afraid of white towels because I assumed they would get dingy and dirty over time, but truly, they are easy to keep white and just feel so fresh and clean in a bathroom. If you want your bathroom to feel like a spa, outfit it with fluffy white towels and use them. Roll them up in a basket or hang them from hooks or a towel bar.

DISPLAY ITEMS YOU USE EVERY DAY

Glass storage jars or apothecary jars can be an attractive way to display those bathroom items you use every day. Cotton swabs, cotton balls and pads, Epsom salts, soaps—if you have room on your counter, put out pretty jars to contain these daily-use items.

TRY AROMATHERAPY

Don't you love a nice-smelling bathroom? I find that one way to keep the room smelling fresh and clean is to make sure you allow your towels to dry thoroughly and keep your bathroom clean during the week. If you want to add a little scent to the room, think of something subtle that reminds you of a spa. I like using essential oils in an electric scent diffuser fitted with a low-wattage bulb to give the bathroom a candle-like glow without the flame.

My favorite blend is equal parts lavender and eucalyptus. I usually put two or three drops of each into the diffuser. It's subtle but soothing.

You could also try changing the scent while you clean the bathroom each week to make the task more pleasant.

ESTABLISH A BATH RITUAL

Want to make your bathroom feel cozy? Create a bath-time ritual that helps you wind down. Turn the lights down, light a candle, use bath salts or bubbles, grab a book you've been meaning to read, and enjoy your clean bathroom.

"BEFORE YOU GO" SPRAY

You know that "before you go" spray you've seen in the store? You can make your own with just four ingredients. Feel free to vary the combination of essential oils.

INGREDIENTS

⅓ cup water

30 drops lemon essential oil

30 drops orange essential oil

½ teaspoon fractionated coconut oil

SPECIAL EQUIPMENT

8-ounce spray bottle

Fractionated coconut oil (available at online retailers; it helps the mixture sit on the surface of the water)

Combine all ingredients in the spray bottle, shake, and spray on the toilet water before you go.

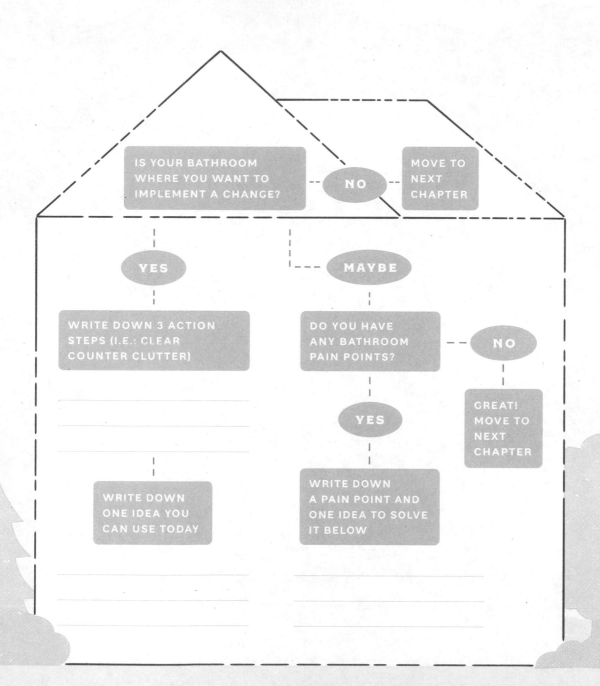

IS YOUR BATHROOM WHERE YOU WANT TO IMPLEMENT A CHANGE?

NO — MOVE TO NEXT CHAPTER

YES

MAYBE

WRITE DOWN 3 ACTION STEPS (I.E.: CLEAR COUNTER CLUTTER)

DO YOU HAVE ANY BATHROOM PAIN POINTS?

NO

GREAT! MOVE TO NEXT CHAPTER

YES

WRITE DOWN ONE IDEA YOU CAN USE TODAY

WRITE DOWN A PAIN POINT AND ONE IDEA TO SOLVE IT BELOW

CHAPTER 12

Bedrooms

IT'S TIME TO MOVE INTO THE BEDROOM, A PLACE THAT WE SHOULD TREAT like a haven at the end of a long day. What are your biggest bedroom stressors? Does the room feel stale? Is it dusty? Is there a perpetual pile of laundry on a chair? Do you stash stuff in your bedroom because no one goes in there anyway? Do you forget to make your bed but appreciate a made bed?

In order to decide what systems and rituals to put into place in the bedroom, you need to determine why this space is causing you stress or discomfort. This should be your soft place to land, not a dumping ground.

We're going to tackle two important areas: first our beds and linens, then our closets and clothes.

Before we get started, I want you to think through the things that aren't working in your bedroom. I'll go first—below are my bedroom Pain Points.

- Unfolded laundry

- Bedroom becomes dusty quickly

- Unmade bed

- Clutter and piles of stuff stashed but not put away
- Dirty clothes on the floor and not in a hamper
- Things under the bed
- Non-clothing items in the closet
- Clothes not accessible
- Holding on to clothing that I no longer wear or that no longer fits
- Not putting things where they belong because I'm rushing
- Clean clothes that aren't put away

Write down a few things that cause you stress or are bothersome in your bedroom.

_____

_____

_____

Do you have more than one bedroom? Use the space below to detail Pain Points in each one.

_____

_____

_____

Do you have a system already in place for any of the things that cause you stress or are even just an annoyance in the bedroom? What have you tried? What do you think might work?

Let's start with the bed and come up with some systems to make it truly the most relaxing place we can fall into at night!

Systems for the Bedroom

PAIN POINT: I Can't Remember to Make the Bed
SOLUTION: Make the Bed as Soon as You Get Up

A made bed is so nice at the end of the day. Figure out how you're going to put this system into place, because it's important. The easiest way I've found is to pair it with something you're already doing—that is, getting up. So as soon as you step out of the bed, make it. If you're the last one out of the bed, make it as soon as you stand up. If you get up before your partner, make the bed after you get dressed for the day.

For example, I always get up an hour or two before my husband does. He will typically pull the covers up when he gets out of bed, but I'll straighten them out and put the pillows on, including extras (he's not a fan of them, but I am!), after I shower and get dressed for the day.

Some people like to pull down the covers and let the bed air out before pulling the covers back up. If that's you, pair bed making with something else you do daily to ensure it gets done.

- **Top sheets are optional.** This tip is one I've followed as long as my husband and I have been married. Why? Because his mom made beds this way, and I quickly discovered that he couldn't deal with a top sheet. At first I found the system odd and wondered if it was really hygienic, but through the years I've adopted it as my own and absolutely love it. My mother-in-law made beds this way because she had an autoimmune disease (her hands and energy level couldn't handle the extra step), but I make beds this way because it's so much easier. It also makes it easier for the kids to make their own beds.

  Consistent sheet washing is what makes this work. I wash sheets and towels on Saturdays and find that all week long the beds are easy to make. It's even quicker to change the sheets—so simple and easy. I don't change the duvet cover every week, but I do change it every other week or every third week.

- **Wash sheets on a designated day of the week.** Choosing a day on which you wash your sheets helps ensure that this task will get done. I like Saturdays because everyone in the house can help out. If you don't want to wash all the bedding weekly, split it up so it's not so overwhelming. Do two beds one week and two the next. The main thing is to make your bed daily and change the sheets regularly. This is a bed-making system.

- **Learn to handle duvet covers.** Here's a trick for getting a clean duvet cover on quickly and easily (like, two to three minutes easy):

  - Turn the duvet cover inside out.

  - Place it on top of the comforter.

- Tie any ties in place (if you have them).

- Grab the top left corner of the cover and pull it over the comforter, repeating with the right side, essentially right-siding it out.

- Pull the cover over the comforter and shake it out a bit and arrange it on the bed.

- **Pillow talk.** While we're talking beds, let's talk pillows. Keep a pillow protector on all your pillows to stave off dust mites. Remove the pillow protector and launder it every other time you wash your bedding. If your pillow feels flat, put it in the dryer for fifteen to thirty minutes on warm and fluff it. Add a few wool dryer balls or clean tennis balls stuffed in socks. The heat from the dryer will kill some germs and refresh the pillow. But don't put a foam or latex pillow in the dryer.

PAIN POINT: The Bedroom Gets So Dusty

SOLUTION: Cover Your Pillows and Mattresses

If the bedroom feels dustier than other areas of the house, it is! With bedding, the mattress, pillows, carpeting (if you have it), and a room that is typically not dusted as frequently, dust can accumulate quickly. One simple solution is to put dust protection on your pillows and mattress. Zip on pillow protectors and a mattress pad—these products put a barrier between you and your pillows and mattress so, assuming you launder your bedding regularly, dust and other allergens stay away from your skin. Launder them frequently to keep the dust down even more.

Also, don't skip weekly dusting and vacuuming in the bedrooms: it's essential to keep the dust at a minimum.

Remove everything possible from the bedroom surfaces and put it in a laundry basket. Dust the surfaces and step back. How does looking at an uncluttered surface make you feel? Then go through your laundry basket and toss, donate, or relocate anything you don't want to keep on display. Put the remaining items back where they were. Take a picture to remind yourself of this clutter-free bedroom and refer back to it if you revert to your old habits.

PAIN POINT: Clothing Seems to Pile Up on Chairs
SOLUTION: Visual Cues

Do you and/or your spouse put clothing on chairs? Maybe your clean clothes start out on your bed, waiting to be folded, only to make their way to a chair because it's time to go to sleep. Or maybe your dirty clothes never quite make their way to the hamper. This is a hard habit to break, but the solution might be as simple as setting up a visual cue reminding you to go just one step further and put these items away. Think of what will work best. If you need a bold reminder, perhaps put up a sign held in place with painter's tape. If a subtle reminder will do, perhaps set out a strategically placed laundry basket. Use your visual cue until you've kicked this habit.

Rituals for Bedrooms

Is there anything you feel is already operating as a Happy Task in your bedroom, especially when it comes to your bed linens? Are there things you enjoy (or at least don't mind) doing when you're there? Write them down in the space below.

SPRITZ THE BEDDING WITH FABRIC SPRAY

Mix up a bottle of my Fabric Refresher and keep it in a basket on your nightstand. If you prefer to air your bed out a bit before making it, pull the bedding back, spritz it, let it air out for an hour or so, then make your bed.

FABRIC REFRESHER

Looking for a safe and effective fabric refresher that eliminates odors and works well on bedding and pillows? This is my favorite! Give your pillow a spritz for a restful night's sleep.

INGREDIENTS

½ cup water

¼ cup vodka or rubbing alcohol

10 drops lavender essential oil

SPECIAL EQUIPMENT

8-ounce spray bottle

Combine all ingredients in the bottle, shake, and spray on any fabric—pillows, bedding, furniture, carpet—that needs a little freshening up.

Grab a pretty basket and use it to store special comfort items you use before bed, such as lotion, lip balm, essential oil, an eye mask, or a book you're reading. Put the basket by your bed to make your nighttime routine feel a little more relaxing.

Systems for Closets

Now let's move on to the closet. What are your biggest clothing and closet stressors? Too many clothes? Not having clean clothes when you need them? Being unable to find the clothes you're looking for? Clothes that are too big or too small taking up space? Not having enough hangers? Storing non-clothing items on the floor or on the shelves? Inadequate shoe storage?

Write down a few things connected with closets and clothing that cause you stress or are bothersome.

QUICK TIP

Keep phones and electronic devices, even televisions, out of your bedroom altogether to encourage a restful ambience. Sometimes it's hard to power down at night, but it's essential if you want to get a good rest and give your body a break from screens.

Now let's look at some systems that can help solve these issues.

How often do you go through your closet to pull out clothes that you no longer wear? Maybe you need a larger size now (and there's no shame in that!). Or maybe you're wearing a smaller size or your style has changed or your season of life has changed: if you used to work in an office but now work from home, you probably don't need a week's worth of business suits. But just determining what to keep and what to donate can be a challenge.

Here's a practice that has worked well for me. Look through the clothes hanging up in your closet, and when you come across something you aren't sure you want to keep, turn the hanger backwards on the rod. Choose a period of time—say, six months—and if you wear the garment within that time and decide you want to keep it, turn the hanger back the right way. If you don't wear it within that time frame, you know it's not something you need to keep, so let it go.

If it's a piece that has an emotional connection for you—say, something your husband gave you for your birthday or something you wore for a special occasion—you can remember how good it made you feel when you received it or wore it, maybe even thank your husband again for his thoughtfulness, then donate it, knowing that it will make someone else feel good when she wears it.

Following are a few ways you can make your closet more organized, which will make it easy to see what you actually have.

- **Sort by color.** Devise a method for hanging up your clothes. For example, group them by color or by type—pants, skirts, jackets, and so on.

- **Use non-slip hangers.** We like using non-slip hangers because they keep clothing in place, take up less space than regular hangers, and give a closet a uniform look and feel.

- **Separate out-of-season clothing.** Do you have a method for separating in-season from out-of-season clothing? Think of the easiest way for you to do this. Maybe you find it helpful to cull your clothing twice a year and choose what is and isn't working for you. Put the "no's" in a donation basket (see below), then put the good stuff in a "keep" box and stash it until the next season.

  At our house, we keep everything out all the time. We live in the Midwest, so we layer a lot, and fortunately, we have the room to do this. But we sort the clothes by type—short sleeve, long sleeve, exercise, pants, jeans.

- **Designate a donation basket.** At my house, everyone's closet has a donation basket: if something no longer fits or has seen better days, it goes in the basket. Once the basket is full, it goes to our favorite donation center. In the kids' closets I keep a bin for the clothes that will be brought down to the basement for storage until the next oldest sibling can grow into it, or it can be given as hand-me-downs to cousins.

This is a great example of a system that, once in place, will make your life much easier. Instead of finding time every few months to weed through all the closets in the house, you can decide as you're trying something on if it's ready to be donated or thrown out.

PAIN POINT: My Closet Is So Disorganized That I Don't Know Where to Start
SOLUTION: Split the Task Up!

There are all sorts of reasons why we put off organizing our clothes. Many things can get in the way: items that don't belong in the closet, clothes on the floor, clothes at the back of the closet, clothes that no longer fit, clothes that have sentimental value but aren't worn, overflowing laundry baskets. If you're feeling overwhelmed by your closet, it's probably because of a combination of these things.

When you're organizing a cupboard or a drawer, I recommend removing everything from it first. But that approach doesn't always work in a cluttered closet. So instead of letting the state of the closet overwhelm you, split up the task by separating it into the following three steps, which don't have to be done all at once.

1. Start by quickly going through the items in your closet and putting anything that you can donate in a basket or bin. Make your first pass quick and ruthless. Bundle up those items and get them out of the room.

2. Then go through the closet one more time and assess a little more strategically. Ask yourself: "Is this something I wear regularly and need to keep? Does it still fit?" By answering those questions, you'll be able to eliminate even more items.

3. Once you've done a dive through the entire closet, separate the items according to type—pants, dresses, short sleeve, long sleeve, and so on (see page 114). As you're sorting, you might find something that you don't need or want anymore—earmark that for your donation basket, too. You might even find a favorite shirt that's been hiding out of sight!

(see page 114)

Keep repeating these three steps until you've organized your closet. If you're still feeling overwhelmed, set a timer for fifteen minutes and work until the timer goes off. Take a break, then go back to it later that day or on another day until you're satisfied.

And remember your tomorrow self—how much is she going to thank you when getting dressed the next morning takes five minutes instead of fifteen because everything is visible, every item fits, and you actually like wearing the clothes you have?

Rituals for Closets

Is there anything you feel is already operating as a Happy Task when it comes to your closet? Are there closet tasks you enjoy (or at least don't mind) doing? Write them down in the space below.

END THE DAY WITH CLOTHING HUNG UP, PUT AWAY, OR IN A HAMPER

Take a quick glance around your bedroom before turning in for the night. Are there any clothes that need to be picked up? This is a simple task that pays big benefits. Make this habit stick by attaching it to a specific time of day instead of walking into the bedroom at night only to find a pile of untouched unfolded laundry on the bed.

Make this an enjoyable ritual by adding a sachet or a sprig of dried lavender to softly scent the closet.

SET OUT CLOTHING THE NIGHT OR WEEK BEFORE

If you struggle in the morning to pick out your clothes, try setting them out the night before. This can be as simple as choosing the clothes and moving the hangers that they are on to the front of the closet, or folding a pile of clothes and placing them where you change in the morning. For example, I'll set out my gym clothes in the evening to ensure that I get up and get right to my workout in the morning.

You can take this one step further: on Saturday, set out clothes for the week as you're folding and hanging them up in the closet. This works really well for kids, too—I do this with my youngest so we don't have any last-minute wardrobe changes before school.

CREATE A CAPSULE WARDROBE

If you feel overwhelmed by how much laundry you do, and by your clothes and closet situation in general, one solution is to create a capsule wardrobe. A capsule wardrobe is a curated collection of clothing that includes timeless, basic pieces that you can mix and match. Having a set number of pieces that you truly love to wear cuts down on the problem of having too many clothes, reduces decision fatigue, and ensures that when you reach for an outfit in the morning, it will be something you actually enjoy wearing. You can even pull outfit ideas from Pinterest or your own closet (take a picture) and put them on an idea board so you have a couple inspirational outfit ideas to use when needed.

When setting up a capsule wardrobe, decide how many items you need and work your way through until you reach your target number. Maybe you want to get your wardrobe down to thirty items. Or maybe you need a specific number of work outfits. Keep only those items that you can easily mix and match. As you're going through your closet, you may find that you own five skirts, yet your favorite pair of jeans is growing threadbare. Use this opportunity to donate the skirts you don't like and invest in another pair of jeans that you'll wear often.

If you need to put some items in a box so you can make a decision about them later, that's fine! Store the box out of the way and put a date on it—anywhere from one month to one year in the future. If you haven't needed or wanted to wear those items within that time period, maybe it's time to donate them. There are plenty of books and online articles about building a capsule wardrobe; if this is something that interests you, I encourage you to check those out!

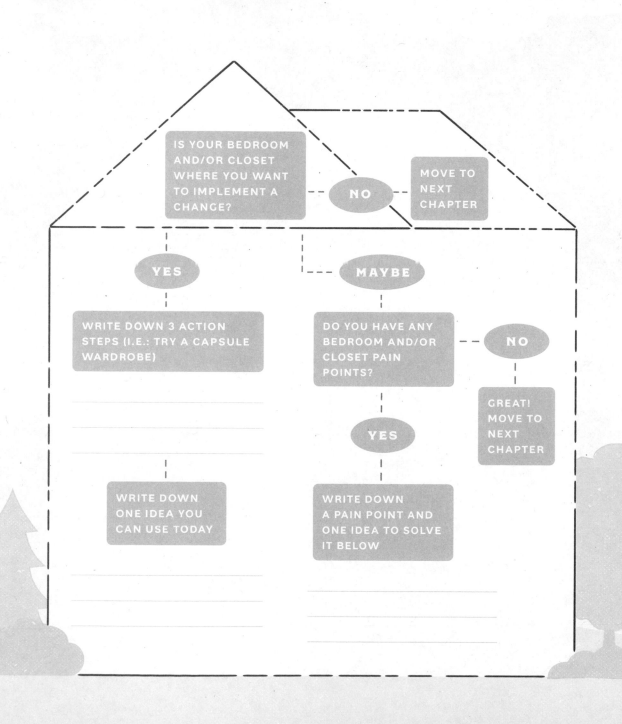

IS YOUR BEDROOM AND/OR CLOSET WHERE YOU WANT TO IMPLEMENT A CHANGE?

NO

MOVE TO NEXT CHAPTER

YES

MAYBE

WRITE DOWN 3 ACTION STEPS (I.E.: TRY A CAPSULE WARDROBE)

DO YOU HAVE ANY BEDROOM AND/OR CLOSET PAIN POINTS?

NO

GREAT! MOVE TO NEXT CHAPTER

YES

WRITE DOWN ONE IDEA YOU CAN USE TODAY

WRITE DOWN A PAIN POINT AND ONE IDEA TO SOLVE IT BELOW

CHAPTER 13

Linens + Laundry

LAUNDRY IS ONE OF THOSE NEVER-ENDING CHORES, WHICH CAN MAKE IT feel especially daunting. As soon as you fold and put away one load, there's another ready to go in the wash. What are your biggest linens-and-laundry stressors? Are you sick of looking at piles of unwashed or washed clothes? Can't remember the last time you washed your sheets?

Nothing screams "I haven't gotten anything done today!" or "I'm totally in over my head!" like a pile of dirty laundry. Honestly, I think this is because it just takes so long. We have an idea in our heads of how long it will take to fold and put away those clothes based on the number of times we've been stuck in a room for hours trying to get caught up with it. Let's elevate our laundry systems and bring a little more joy to the clothes-washing process.

In order to decide what systems and rituals to put in place when it comes to laundry, you need to determine *what* is causing you stress and why you aren't loving the process.

I'll go first—below are my laundry Pain Points.

- Spilled detergent (powder and liquid)
- Bunched-up sheets

- Mismatched linens

- Laundry piles

Use the space below to write down a few things that cause you stress or are bothersome when it comes to your linens and laundry.

_____

_____

_____

_____

Do you have a system already in place for any of the things that cause stress or are even just an annoyance when you're doing laundry? What have you tried? What do you think might work?

Systems for Laundry

PAIN POINT: Doing My Family's Laundry Takes Forever
SOLUTION: Improved System for Doing Family Laundry

It might feel silly to try to come up with a system for doing laundry, but I'm here to tell you that this just may become your favorite of all the ones you put in place. Having a plan helps you know what needs to be laundered when by using specific "rules" to guide you in accomplishing this seemingly overwhelming task. Don't skip over this system—give it a couple minutes of thought, and watch your clothes almost fold themselves.

- **Wash family members' clothes on designated days.** Each family member has a particular day of the week when his or her clothes will be laundered.

- **Use a divided hamper.** My husband and I have a three-compartment hamper in our bedroom closet. One section is for him, one is for me, and the third is for hand towels.

- **Provide each kid with his or her own laundry basket.** Put one small laundry basket in each kid's room. This is a great way to teach your kids to do laundry (and enlist their help). If you use small laundry baskets, there will be fewer clothes to wash and put away, which is less overwhelming for kids as they learn.

- **Minimize the number of sheets you have for each bed.** Do you need three sets of queen-size sheets when you only have one queen-size bed? Probably not. Assess what you have and determine whether you have any worn sheets that can be repurposed or donated. (Many donation centers recycle fabric items such as sheets and towels. They can take them even if they're worn.)

- **Store sheet sets together.** Fold your sheets as neatly as you can and store them in a pillowcase. Stack the sets on a shelf or in a basket for easy access. No more bundled-up sheets, and the sets stay together. The best thing about this? It's okay if your fitted sheets aren't perfectly folded because they hide in the pillowcase.

- **Wash sheets and towels on Saturdays.** I wash my sheets and towels on Saturdays because other family members are home and can help—and because I want my kids to know how to put sheets on a bed when they leave the nest.

- **Wash cleaning cloths and kitchen towels on Saturdays.** Once the sheets and towels go from the washer to the dryer, I wash a load of cleaning cloths on the hottest water cycle with ¼ cup of white vinegar and laundry soap. Then the washer, too, is clean and ready for the next week.

- **Do at least one load of laundry a day.** This might feel more like a chore than a system right now, but if you have the right mind-set, it can become a ritual. Sit down, turn on a podcast or a show, relax, and fold that load of clothes. Put them away, then tomorrow, pick up the show or podcast where you left off.

PAIN POINT: Folding Is the Worst!
SOLUTION: Better Folding Methods

Clothing, bedding, and towels all fall into the category of things that get folded or hung up. I recommend that you come up with a folding method that works for your family, your laundry system, and where you're storing these items. There isn't a right or wrong way to fold things, but it does help if there is a system for how they are stored. It takes the guesswork out of the process and makes it just a bit easier and nicer to look at—not to mention easier to find what you're looking for.

My method for folding is on pages 127 to 129; try it out (or try a version of it that works for you) and watch your shelves and drawers become neat and tidy.

WASH AT LEAST ONE LOAD
OF LAUNDRY A DAY

Doing a load of laundry a day takes a little bit of work on the front end, and it might take you a week or two to get used to the mind shift it requires, but I guarantee you'll wonder how you did laundry any other way once you get the system working for you. Doing a load of laundry daily is a huge part of feeling caught up, less overwhelmed, and in control of this seemingly never-ending household task. Here are some tips that make this work for me:

• **Collect the laundry the night before.** First, collect all the laundry in the house at the end of the day. Keep a hamper in the laundry room and wash what's in that daily. With three kids, I easily have enough to do a load of laundry every day, and some days there are multiple loads.

• **Set up a kids' clothing system.** Don't separate the kids' clothes into lights and darks—just toss it all in and wash it in cold water: I've never had any issues with color transfer. Older kids can fold their own clothes and put them away.

Also, when they're home over the summer, you can teach your kids how to do their own laundry from start to finish.

• **Set up an adults' clothing system.** I do recommend separating adult clothes into lights, darks, and workout wear. In my house, my husband and I each have our own section of the hamper so I can wash our clothes separately. We both work out quite a bit, so I usually have a load of workout clothes for each of us weekly, too.

• **Use the timer on your washing machine.** If you have a washer that allows you to set a specific start time, use it. If you work outside the home, set your washer to start an hour or so before you get up in the morning. Once you get up, toss the wet clothes in the dryer and fold them before leaving for the day or after you get home.

• **Get caught up.** Use the following techniques when you get behind or if you

continued

prefer to do your laundry weekly. And if you don't have enough laundry for a load each day, try doing a load every other day or every third day.

Gather all the laundry in the house and put the baskets or hampers in the laundry room. My recommendation is to wash the adult clothes first, followed by (in order) the kids' clothes, bedding, bath towels, kitchen towels, and cleaning cloths and rags.

Line the baskets up in order of what's going in the washing machine from first to last. If you have a "quick wash" option on your washing machine, this is the time to use it.

Start with adult clothes—don't sort, just combine lights and darks into one load, and wash everything in cold water.

Next, do one load per child—no sorting; all of it goes in a single load and gets washed in cold water. Depending on how much laundry there is and on the capacity of your machines, you can combine these loads into one, but for sorting's sake it's probably easier to wash each child's clothes separately.

After all the clothing has been washed, it's time for bedding. Then move on to bath towels, hand towels, and bath mats. Wash, fold, and put it all away. Take the extra second or two to make sure you're putting everything away neatly; it'll be worth it as you continue.

Finally, wash your kitchen towels and cleaning cloths or rags. Fold these and put them away.

While each load is washing and drying, fold, hang, and put away the previous load as soon as it comes out of the dryer. If you can't finish it all, put the rest off until the next day. If you have a lot of laundry, divide the task into two days.

Once you're finished with all your washing, put your washer on a "clean" cycle or simply run it on the hottest water setting. Select the "extra rinse" option and add ¾ cup of white vinegar **or** ¾ cup of non-chlorine bleach (not both!) to the bleach dispenser or washtub and fill it to its maximum level. Allow the cycle to run until it has completed. Open the top and let the washer air- dry. If you have a front-loading or HE (high-efficiency) washing machine, you will want to keep the door open in between loads to allow it to dry completely.

Sheets

- Pull the sheets out of the dryer. Try to get them when they're still warm so you don't have wrinkled sheets.

- Fold top sheets in half the long way before you fold them horizontally.

- To fold a fitted sheet, tuck one corner into the other, making a pocket; fold the sheet in half again lengthwise, with the fitted corners on the inside; fold the sheet in half horizontally, bringing the two corners together; then fold in half lengthwise again—it should be about 11 by 14 inches. If not, fold it again.

- Place a pillowcase (or pillowcases, if you use more than two per set of sheets) on top of the sheets and slide all the pieces into the remaining pillowcase. Then fold the pillowcase "flap" under the linens inside it. Now you have a neat package that you can place on a shelf.

- Place the sheet sets on top of each other on a shelf or in a basket.

Towels

- Lay a clean, dry towel on a large surface. Smooth it out.

- Fold the towel in thirds lengthwise.

- If it's a bath towel, fold it in thirds horizontally.

- For your hand towels and washcloths, repeat the first two steps, but fold them in half horizontally rather than in thirds unless you need to fold them that way to fit your storage space.

- **Shorts.** Fold shorts in half lengthwise, then fold them in half horizontally and stack or stand them on end in drawers.

- **Jeans + pants.** Fold kids' pants in half lengthwise. Fold in half horizontally, then in half again, and stack or stand them on end in drawers.

  My husband folds his jeans and pants in half lengthwise, putting a crease in the front, then he folds them horizontally in thirds and stacks them on a shelf in our closet.

  I fold my jeans and pants in half lengthwise and hang them up.

- **T-shirts.** Most T-shirts are hung on hangers in our house—we have the room to do this, and I'm not a fan of fold lines on shirts. When we do fold them, we stand them on end in a drawer if there's room or stack them on top of each other if there isn't.

  When I fold a T-shirt, I hold it up, fold the sleeves and about a third of each side in, lay it flat facedown, then fold it in half and then in half again. If you're looking for a perfect fold, you can always try a shirt folder, but I find it quicker just to fold by hand.

- **Leggings.** Fold leggings in half lengthwise and then in half horizontally. I continue to fold horizontally until the leggings are folded to be about as small as the waistband. Then I stand them on end in my drawer—this is the only way they fit.

- **Pajamas.** I like to make a "package" with pajama sets. This makes it easy to grab the set, and it eliminates the search for matching pieces. I start by folding the pants in half lengthwise, then in half horizontally. Then I fold the top's sleeves inward and place the pants in the bottom half of the top. Then I fold the top half of the top over, making a pajama package.

- **Socks.** We do socks differently for everyone in the house. I fold my socks in half horizontally, then open the top of one sock and bring the band over both socks so they form a neat ball. This is the only way they fit in my narrow sock drawer.

  My husband keeps his socks in baskets in our closet—one for sport socks and one for dress socks. Nothing gets matched or folded.

  Each kid has a bin in his or her top drawer next to an undies bin, and the socks get tossed in there. I buy large packs of identical socks so there is very little matching necessary. Grab undies and two socks and go.

- **Undies.** Fold in half, then in half again. Stack them and place them in a drawer if you're feeling fancy. I prefer storing my undies in a small bin in the top drawer of my dresser so I can just toss them in. Simple, easy, and no fuss.

PAIN POINT: Disorganized Linen Closet
SOLUTION: Fold Items in a Uniform Way and Group Them Together

---

An organized linen closet is lovely to look at, but because the items in it are typically not all the same size, and because it's often a small space, it's frequently neglected or overlooked. If your linen closet is stuffed to the brim, you want to do two things: eliminate excess items and fold everything in a uniform manner so it all fits on the shelves and can be seen at a glance. Try the following method to organize your linen closet once and for all. If you don't have a linen closet, you can store your linens in a bathroom cupboard, an armoire, or a dresser.

INVENTORY

Start by removing everything from the closet. Then group like items together—bath towels together, queen-size sheets together, twin-size sheets together. Wipe down the shelves and surfaces.

EDIT

Once everything is grouped together, make sure it's good enough to keep. For example, if you have twelve sets of sheets and only two beds in your house, you probably have too many sets of sheets. I keep only two sets of sheets per bed.

If you see something that's tattered or worn out, put it in a donate pile. Take this editing one step further and decide if there are items in good condition that you don't use or need anymore. Move those to a donate pile as well. If you notice you need to replace something, make a note.

FOLD AND PUT AWAY

Once you've determined what you're going to keep, group like items together and fold them in a uniform manner (see pages 127–129). Stack them together, then slide them back into your linen closet. We keep sheet sets and pillows in our teeny-tiny linen closet, but we keep towels in our bathroom cupboards. Consider a basket or shelf divider if you need a little more structure.

PAIN POINT: Removing Stains

SOLUTION: Ready-to-Go Stain Removal Kit

You know there will be stains you'll have to remove, so let's set up a little stain removal kit and keep it in the laundry room. Below is a list of the items you'll need.

- Spray bottle filled with filtered water

- Powdered oxygen whitener

- Bar of castile soap

- Small soft scrub brush

- Clean white cloth for blotting

I've found that most stains will come out if quickly blotted when the stain occurs, which will pull it out. Then, spray the stain with water and sprinkle oxygen whitener on it. Next, gently rub it with the scrub brush. Alternatively, rub the stain with a bar of castile soap. Either of these methods can be used, after which the item can be laundered as usual. Put the supplies in a cute basket, and store it on a shelf or on top of the dryer

Rituals for Laundry + Linens

Laundry feels like a chore when it's piled up and looks like mountains of work, but if you have a method and a system for getting it done, and if you pair it with a ritual or two, it's much easier and might just feel enjoyable.

Is there anything you feel is already operating as a Happy Task in your laundry room? Are there things you enjoy (or at least don't mind) doing when you're there? Write them down in the space below.

_____

_____

_____

_____

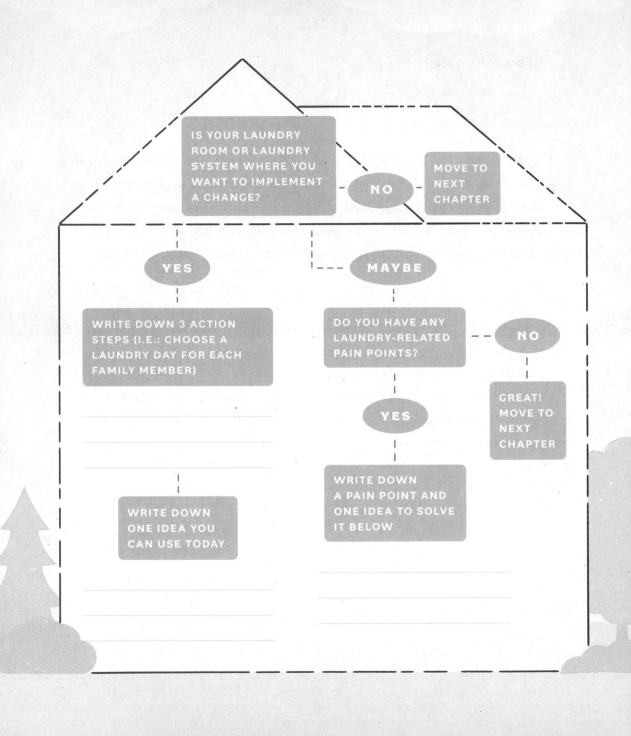

PUT A LAUNDRY BASKET NEXT TO THE WASHING MACHINE FOR LINE-DRY ITEMS

This simple ritual extends the life of your clothes and might make you feel like a laundry rock star. As I move the clothes from the washer to the dryer, I put a laundry basket next to the washer. I put anything that needs to be line-dried in the basket and continue to load the dryer. Once the dryer is whirring away, I turn my attention to the line-dry items and hang them up. No more shrinkage.

FOLD LAUNDRY RIGHT OUT OF THE DRYER

Take your clean clothes out of the dryer and put them in a basket, then bring the basket to a comfortable place where you can fold them. But do it right away: putting off this task can lead to wrinkles, and not wanting to do the laundry. I find that if I take the clothes straight from the warm dryer and put them on our bed, it's easier for me to fold and put them away promptly than if I leave the basket for later. If I leave it for later, later means a lot later. Like, the next day, maybe. That's why I've built this into a ritual—so I can enjoy it just a wee bit. Not to mention the feel of those warm, sweet-smelling clothes as I fold them.

CHOOSE SHEETS AND TOWELS YOU TRULY LOVE

Choose sheets and towels you love—they should make you feel pampered. I love white sheets and towels because I can wash them in hot water with a scoop or two of oxygen whitener to brighten them up. I also prefer 100 percent cotton percale sheets, but it you like microfiber or flannel or something else, get what you love. Folding scratchy sheets and brittle towels is no fun (neither is using them!), so buying items that you love and feel nice as you handle them will help make this a more pleasant task.

MAKE LAUNDRY A TREAT FOR THE SENSES!

Use essential oils that smell nice as you're doing laundry. Set up a small diffuser in your laundry space, add a couple drops to wool dryer balls, or scent your white vinegar with essential oil for use as your fabric softener. Put on music or a podcast, especially while you're folding, which will help pass the time and make the chore less onerous. Enlist other family members to help whenever possible. And if you're simply looking for a little alone time, chances are you'll find it when there's laundry to be folded (ha!).

CHAPTER 14

Living Spaces

THE TERM "LIVING SPACES" MIGHT REFER TO A FAMILY ROOM, LIVING ROOM, rec room, den, or any area where you spend time "living." Think for a minute about the purpose of such a space. In the kitchen, the purpose is food storage and preparation (and sometimes eating). In the bathroom it's hygiene. Living spaces look different from family to family, but most of us view them as places where we can spend time together, relax, watch movies, play games, and read. Are your living spaces working as they should? Are you able to relax and enjoy the comfort of your living spaces? Or are they filled with clutter? Are the surfaces loaded down? Do the objects on them have breathing room?

In order to decide what systems and rituals to put into place in your living spaces, you need to determine *what* is causing you stress and why you aren't loving your living spaces. Once we get to the bottom of that, we'll fine-tune the systems and rituals.

I'll go first—following are my Pain Points in our living spaces.

- Clutter

- Unread magazines

- Socks left on the floor and sofas

- Dog toys scattered everywhere

- Pillows and blankets not put away

- Reading material left out

- Games not put away

- Toys left out

Write down a few things that cause you stress or are bothersome in your living spaces.

_____

_____

_____

_____

Do you have more than one living space? Use the space below to detail Pain Points in each one.

_____

_____

_____

_____

Do you have a system already in place for any of the things that cause stress or are even just an annoyance in your living spaces? What have you tried? What do you think might work?

Systems for Living Spaces

PAIN POINT: Cluttered Surfaces

SOLUTION: Clear Only One Surface at a Time

This is such a quick and easy mood booster! If you're not sure where to start in your living area but feel overwhelmed, try this: just clear one surface.

- Identify a surface to clear. This can be an end table, a coffee table, a mantel, or even the floor.

- Completely clear it. Leave *nothing* on the surface.

- Wipe the surface off with a barely damp cloth and/or your favorite cleaner. Step back and gaze at that clean and empty surface. Sometimes a clean and clear surface can give a little calm to a room. Leave it empty for a bit if you can.

- When you're ready, evaluate what you're going to put back. Remember: part of making long-term changes is being aware of what's working and what isn't. Do you need everything that used to be on that surface? Are you using those things daily or weekly? Is there anything you can donate, sell, or put somewhere else?

- Return the necessities to the surface. Evaluate the surface again—how does it look? Do you want to make any additional edits?

Cleaning and clearing surfaces in the living area gives us room to really *be* in the room, and it allows us to relax and enjoy the space without clutter giving us an uneasy, stressed-out feeling.

If you're feeling inspired, go ahead and clean and clear other surfaces in your living space. It makes a big difference, and it keeps only the things that you love and use often out in the open.

PAIN POINT: Disorganized Books and Magazines
SOLUTION: Organize Like a Pro

BOOKS

Books are wonderful (case in point: thanks for reading this one!), but they can easily turn into clutter if we don't have a good system for organizing them. Bookcases and coffee tables are the most obvious places to store books. Here are some ideas for storing them that will make them organized *and* pretty.

- Arrange by author or title

- Arrange by color—blue books together, red books together, green books together, and so on

- Make a rainbow on your shelf—group books in the order of the visible spectrum (red, orange, yellow, green, blue, indigo, and violet)

- Organize by genre, as bookstores do (e.g., mysteries, memoirs, home decor books, and so on)

- Place some of your books spine out and others face out (to show off those gorgeous jackets and covers)

- Turn your books backwards so all you see is a sea of white and cream pages (although beautiful, this system will make it difficult to find what you're looking for)

Ultimately, do what you love, so you can look at your books and be reminded of why you have them in the first place.

MAGAZINES

I love magazines, but it's easy for them to pile up, get scattered about, and ultimately feel like clutter—just another stack of outdated paper that you have to deal with. Following are some ways to keep on top of your magazines.

- I keep our magazines in a basket on the coffee table in our family room as well as in a basket on top of our bookcase. I also added a second basket on the coffee table to hold the ones I'm currently working through.

- Decide which magazines to keep and for how long. At the end of that fixed period of time, recycle them.

- If you collect certain magazines and want to keep every issue, consider buying stand-up magazine files so you can keep them in chronological order.

- Maybe you like to tear out inspiring images, recipes, or articles from your magazines. All you need are two binders with plastic sleeves. Put the recipes in one and the inspiration in the other.

- Want to eliminate the paper but keep some of the articles? Scan or photograph your favorite magazine clippings and save the images to your computer or tablet.

TOY STORAGE

If you have kids, you most likely have toys in your living spaces. Your feeling about this can go from "It's nice to have toys here for the kids to play with while I'm cooking or doing something else" to "It looks like a toy store threw up in here." Let's find a way for both you and your kids to be happy with the toy situation. Below are my tips.

- **Provide adequate storage.** I like baskets and soft storage for holding toys. Look for open baskets with handles that can be easily accessed. Baskets also look pretty on a shelf if you are storing toys in an area with a multiple purpose. You might also consider a lidded container that you can store on a shelf or stowed away in a closet. The main idea is that you provide a way for toys to be cleaned up, stored easily, *and* look pretty when everything is put away.

- **Think in reverse.** As you come up with a system for toy storage, ask yourself the following question: What will this space look and feel like when everything is dumped out of the container on the floor and strewn from one end of the room to the other? How long will it take to clean up? Is there too much in the container? Are things difficult to locate? Are there too many options for playtime? It's important to minimize the frustration—for kids and for you—when it comes to cleaning things up.

- **Devise a rotating storage system.** You don't need to have every toy your kids own out in the open at the same time. In fact, I find that a rotating toy system both helps keep toy clutter at bay *and* gets the kids excited to play with toys that they haven't seen in a while. Keep some toys in a toy storage location (a closet, basement, attic, under their bed, etc.). Rotate toy bins as you see fit—you might have three bins that you rotate through, or you may have fifteen. Do what works best for your home. The idea is that the toys remain fresh, and more meaningful play can occur because there are fewer choices and fewer toys. Clean up time is easier too!

- **Identify toy storage areas with the kids.** Make sure everything has a home and that your kids know what it is. Label containers with pictures or words, and show your kids how and where to put things away. Making labels can be as simple as finding the image of the toy online, copy/pasting it into a document, printing it out, and laminating it. Take this label and attach it to the outside of the bin or basket for easy identification. If your kids are anything like mine, showing them once will not be enough—you'll need to reinforce the system you create. Adjust it when necessary and encourage them to put things away when they're done playing with them.

- **Manage pet toys.** You might also have pets who have their own toys strewn about. Follow a similar system, and you'll no longer be tripping over squeaky toys.

BLANKET STORAGE

If you have blankets or throws in your living areas, make sure you have just enough of them and not too many. If you have a few extras that aren't pulled out all the time, consider placing them in a basket or—my favorite—rolling them up in a large antique stoneware crock that sits on the floor next to the sofa. You could also put them in a drawer until you need them.

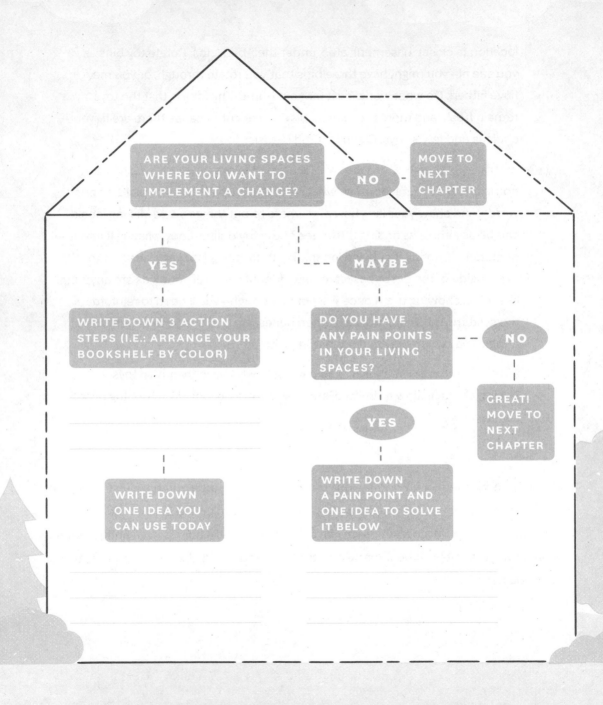

Rituals for Living Spaces

Following are some ideas for turning your living spaces into welcoming, relaxing places where you and your family can spend time together.

But before we get started, is there anything you feel is already operating as a Happy Task in your living spaces? Are there things you enjoy (or at least don't mind) doing when you're there? Write them down in the space below.

_____

_____

_____

_____

TIMER GAME

Living areas can get messy in a hurry. But cleaning them up doesn't have to be a chore. Instead, make it a game! Set a timer for five minutes and race to do a quick pickup. Put on music and make it fun. If you have little ones, get them involved, too. They'll need help, but they can definitely learn to put their toys back. Even though my kids are no longer little, I still do a nightly cleanup with them. I'll even set a timer for myself and see how much I can get done—this trick works for all ages.

SET THE MOOD WITH MUSIC + LIGHTING

Make your living space inviting by turning on some music—make a family playlist of your favorites and set the mood. Dim the overhead lights and turn on the table lamps and floor lamps. Light some candles and fill a diffuser with some pleasing scents. This sets the tone for the whole home and will help your family feel cozy and comfortable in the space.

PUT GAMES AND BOOKS OUT
TO ENCOURAGE INTERACTION

If you want to change how your living areas are being used, set out a few puzzles, games, and books, all of which encourage interaction and can have an effect on the mood and the room.

THROW A PARTY

There's no better way to enjoy your living areas and make your hard work seem worthwhile than enjoying them with other people. Have some guests over and take pride in your space. Remember: it doesn't have to be perfectly organized or decorated to be welcoming.

CHAPTER 15

Office + Paperwork

PAPERWORK: IT SOUNDS SO DULL AND BORING, BUT IT'S ONE OF THE MOST insidious clutter producers in the home. Whether you have a dedicated home office, a desk or table that doubles as a place to pay bills, a table that *became* a home office while you were unexpectedly working from home, or just a coffee table that's piling up with mail, you almost certainly have a paper problem.

Think about all the kids' drawings, the photos, the permission slips, the calendars, the bills, and, of course, the mail. What snags do you run into when it comes to paper in your home? Are you worried that you won't be able to find something important? Want to get started but feel like the project would take too long and you don't want to have papers strewn from one end of the room to the other? Getting buried in piles of bills that you can't bring yourself to cope with?

In order to decide what systems and rituals for dealing with paperwork to put into place, you need to determine *what* is causing you stress and why you aren't loving your office or wherever your paperwork lives. Once we get to the bottom of that, we'll fine-tune your paperwork systems and rituals.

I'll go first—following are my Pain Points when it comes to paperwork and paper clutter.

- Stacks of paper

- Not being able to find an important document

- Getting behind on paperwork

- Setting aside time to sort and file

- Wanting to digitize things but not having or making the time to do so

Write down a few things that cause you stress or are bothersome when it comes to paperwork and paper clutter.

_____

_____

_____

Do you have any systems in place for dealing with papers and paperwork? Is this a pain point for you? What have you tried? What do you think might work?

Systems for Paperwork

PAIN POINT: Disorganized Mail
SOLUTION: Set Up a Mail Station

Mail can be overwhelming, and trust me, you're not the only one who feels like it's impossible to get ahead of the never-ending pile. In fact, mail is one of the biggest problem areas for us all, and every week I get hundreds of requests on my blog for help with taming the mail beast.

That's because mail comes six days a week, and if you have kids, you also have school-related mail coming in five days a week. On top of that, we get dozens, if not hundreds, of pieces of digital mail every day in the form of emails and texts that pour into our in-boxes and phones every day. It's a barrage of information—no wonder we feel constantly overloaded!

So let's take this major Pain Point and turn it into a much less painful system that will work almost automatically to keep your mail under control.

First let me tell you the *real* secret to mail: deal with it right away. Process it as soon as it crosses the threshold, but if that's not possible, try to set aside a few minutes each night to tackle it. Most important, have a place for everything.

To start, we're going to put some good habits to work so the mail doesn't pile up.

Step 1 is to divide the stack of mail that's staring you down into the following categories:

- Junk mail

- Bills

- Magazines and catalogs

- Invitations and anything that requires a response

- Coupons

Then, once you have everything separated, go through the categories and take the following steps. You may want to open your mail over a shredder, recycling bin, or garbage can so you can immediately get rid of whatever you don't need.

- **Junk mail.** Recycle or shred.

- **Bills.** Open, then recycle or shred unnecessary inserts and the outer envelope. Place the bill itself, along with the reply envelope, in a dedicated basket or folder.

- **Magazines and catalogs.** Recycle or throw out what you don't want. Keep only what you know you will read within thirty days. Store whatever's left over in a basket or bin, and once a month, empty the whole basket and recycle anything you haven't cracked open.

- **Invitations and anything that requires a response.** Open, toss the outer envelope, then put in a to-do pile. Set a digital reminder to respond later.

- **Coupons.** Store in an envelope, folder, or small accordion file. Once a month, throw out expired coupons and those you no longer plan to use.

Now that you have that stack of mail dealt with, it's time to set up a mail station.

HOW TO SET UP A MAIL STATION

Creating a space where you can drop your mail, pay your bills, and hold important invitations or forms is an important step toward having fewer paper piles and a more organized household. First decide what kinds of items you want to keep in your mail station. And although there's nothing wrong with having pretty office supplies, this isn't about finding an excuse to buy things—all we really want to do is make sure the system is functional. Think hard about what you'll actually use every day.

Following are some ideas.

- Manila folders or envelopes labeled with categories such as TO PAY, TO FILE, INVITATIONS, SCHOOL, IN PROCESS
- Pens and pencils
- Stapler and paper clips
- Calendar
- Stamps
- Checkbook
- Calculator
- Paper shredder

- Letter opener
- Phone charger
- Address and phone book

- Catchall container (for your lip balm, nail clipper, keys, extra garage door opener, wallet)

Next, decide where you'll place the mail and other paperwork when it comes in. It can be as simple as a basket by the door as you are getting started, but eventually you will probably want a mail sorter or system that can help you keep things organized and in place. You just want one spot where the stack of mail will be put the second it's brought in so that it doesn't end up in a pile where it doesn't belong. Set something up that's easy for any family member to access and encourage family members and kids to empty mail and paper from their bags into this spot as soon as they walk into the house. A sweet note by the door will go far in helping them remember to unpack before they get distracted.

Once you've established where your mail station will be, then you'll want to figure out how to reduce the amount of unwanted paper you receive.

Following are a few sites and resources I've found that will help you cut down on junk mail.

- **DMAChoice.** If you go to the website dmachoice.org, you can select what types of direct mail you want to receive and what you don't want to receive.

- **Catalog Choice.** This is a free service (sign up at CatalogChoice.org) that allows you to opt out of catalogs, coupons, credit card offers, phone books, circulars, and more. (This is also a great way to reduce the temptation to buy things you don't need!)

- **Magic Envelope.** This is a service, available at Shoeboxed.com, that sends you a postage-paid envelope that you fill with receipts and other papers you want to be digitized. If you really never want to deal with paper again, this could be your way out!

- **PaperKarma.** This service allows you to snap a photo of your junk mail, send it to the company, and it will handle unsubscribing you: find out more at PaperKarma.com.

BILL PAYING

Can bill paying be enjoyable? For me, it's not as bad as it used to be now that I have a system and I'm not paying bills late. Decide if bill paying is a task you need to do weekly, biweekly, or monthly. Chances are your choice will be based on when you have money coming in and when your bills are due.

Sit down and get real with your finances—what's coming in, what's going out—and set up a system for taking care of your bills. Are you saving for something? Getting out of debt? Or just trying to avoid late fees? A lot of issues around money can be resolved just by sitting down with your finances regularly and figuring out exactly where you stand.

Schedule your bill-paying time on the calendar and try it out. If it doesn't work, try another schedule. Do you need a system for keeping track of bills and accounts? A bill-paying notebook or an app can help. I've found that keeping track of finances on paper is helpful for some because you can reference the information quickly and easily, and it's right in front of you—you're forced to see your finances at a glance.

ELECTRONIC BANKING

We do our banking electronically, and I've found that the best way to stay on top of it is to set up automatic payments and check our accounts daily. That way I can move money around or check on bills and payments with the click of a finger. Electronic bill paying isn't really a "set it and forget it" system, but with a quick daily check-in, it works!

Still, I prefer to receive my bills on paper for two reasons: first, otherwise I would have to remember to log in to my various accounts and check them monthly, whereas it's much more efficient for me to have a paper copy to check when it comes in the mail; and second, I can use the paper bill as a cross-reference. I keep the paper bill until it's paid, then I put it in that month's file folder in case I need to use it for tax purposes. Then at the end of the year I give those files to my accountant, and the rest gets shredded.

PAIN POINT: Kids' School Papers and Artwork
SOLUTION: Establish a Storage System

You know that dreaded feeling when the kids go back to school and the papers start to flood in? Or when the kids come home during the last week of school and everything they've done over the course of the year starts coming home with them? It's overwhelming, even though it's expected. So instead of letting myself get buried in the onslaught of paper, I set up a simple method for filing papers and artwork as they come in. This keeps things from getting out of hand.

I have three kids—one in elementary school, one in middle school, and one in high school. My system has been in place for around ten years, and I can tell you that it works with all three of them. You should also know that I was an art teacher for almost ten years, so I have a true love for kids' artwork—especially artwork by my own kids. However, I also know we'd be buried in finger-painted masterpieces if we kept every single thing they made, so I decided to set limits.

But please remember that there isn't one "right" way to handle your kids' creations—their artwork is just as unique as they are! But below is what has worked for my family, and it should provide a strong baseline for building a system that works for yours.

- Keep anything that has a handprint or fingerprints.

- Limit the amount of what you keep to just one box, folder, or other storage container per child. In my home, each kid gets a hanging file folder at the start of every school year.

- Sort through what you're going to keep. Do this with your kids so that pieces important to both of you are kept and so that tears aren't shed later over the loss of a beloved macaroni necklace.

Brainstorm and write down your own system for school papers and artwork in the space below.

_____

_____

_____

_____

Once you've determined what's worth keeping and what nobody will miss, you'll want to keep it all organized and contained. Of course, you don't need to purchase anything for this—repurpose boxes and bins if you want—but I've found that the following three items are really great for keeping everything sorted and ordered.

- **Stackable letter tray.** This is where we keep the daily stuff—anything that needs to be filed, filled out, or given attention soon. Each kid has his or her own file and is in charge of what's in it. I help the kids sort through it when it gets full or if we're on the hunt for a permission slip that needs signing.

  Why this works: It gives in-process papers a home and keeps them off the counters and out of the bottoms of backpacks.

- **Covered file box.** Each kid gets a covered file box that contains fourteen hanging folders—one for each year from kindergarten through twelfth grade. I bought red, yellow, and blue hanging folders, so each kid has his or her own color. This is where we put special papers, things with handprints, grades, and other items we want to keep. Usually during the first week of summer we go through the folder together and assess what we want to keep for the long term. I paste each kid's school picture on the front of every year's folder so there's a running record of how they've grown. These folders get skinnier each year as the kids bring home less paper and we keep less of it.

  Why this works: It forces us to keep just a small selection of favorites and cull them throughout the year. Someday the kids might not want what's in them at all, but in the short term, it's fun for us to sit and look through them a couple of times a year.

- **Portfolio.** There's always artwork that's too big or bulky to put in file boxes, so each kid has a giant archival-quality portfolio that's stored under the bed or in the closet. This is for those precious large pictures and artwork.

  Why this works: Sometimes the hardest-to-store pieces are the most meaningful, so it's essential to figure out a good way to keep them (and keep them out of the way). I'm sure in ten years we won't hold on to everything in the portfolios, but for the time being I like having them to look at, and the kids enjoy going back through the years via their artwork.

Rituals for Paperwork

Is there anything you feel is already operating as a Happy Task in the office or wherever you process your paperwork? Are there things you enjoy (or at least don't mind) doing when you're there? Write them down in the space provided on the following page.

SET ASIDE INTENTIONAL TIME TO PLAN YOUR SCHEDULE

Taking a few minutes to plan out your days, weeks, and months can help you feel in control of what's coming. And adding something pleasurable to the task makes it enjoyable. This is especially helpful if you're the kind of person who gets to the end of the day and wonders where the time went and what you did during all those hours. When you have it written down beforehand, you can see it in front of you.

First think about the time of day that's going to be most effective for your planning. Some people work best first thing in the morning, when their brains are fresh, while others prefer the end of the workday, before they wrap up for the night. Pick a day and a time—say, Monday mornings at seven—then set yourself up for success. The night before, put out what you'll need—your calendar, a pen, and anything else you can think of.

Find a planner or calendar that makes sense for you—look for something with a style you're attracted to and a format that makes sense to you. If you work outside the home and have several appointments each day, you might prefer a daily planner. If you like to see your week at a glance, you'll probably prefer a weekly planner. Maybe you don't want to hassle with paper at all and prefer to sync everything up with your spouse and kids through an app. Or maybe you're a die-hard wall-calendar planner. Me? I'm not an all-in-one-place person—I use a hybrid of my Homekeeping Planner (which you can find at cleanmama.net) and a dry-erase monthly calendar for work and a paper family calendar in the kitchen. I love the flexibility and the fact that my kids and husband don't have to ask me what's going on on Sunday: they just peek at the wall calendar.

When it's time to sit down and plan out the coming day or week, start by making a cup of coffee or tea. Burn a scented candle or put some essential oils in your diffuser, then take a deep breath. It may feel daunting at first, but when you get into the rhythm of doing this on a regular basis, you'll find the peace that comes from knowing what to expect and what you need to plan ahead for. You can even build in free time to your schedule and use it either as a catchall or a chance to relax and spend time with family and friends.

KEEP A JOURNAL

Keeping a journal can be a great way to slow down, take stock of what's going on, get in touch with how you're feeling, and enjoy some time to yourself. You can use something as simple as a lined notebook and put a date at the top of each page or entry. Or you can go as far as to start a bullet journal (read about this method at BulletJournal.com). Jot down the events of the day (or what's on tap for the day), things you are grateful for, a daily to-do list, ideas you want to keep track of, and big and little goals. Pair this ritual with a morning, midday, or evening routine so that writing in this bound stack of paper becomes something special.

ARCHIVE YOUR PHOTOS

If you can't seem to find the time to catch up on photo albums or scrapbooks, start by going through the photos on your phone and deleting those you deem unimportant or unnecessary. Then upload the ones you want to keep to an online storage platform. I also like to back up photos on my hard drive and organize them by month and year. An unexpected pleasure of this system is that you can look up what happened on a given date in the past. My kids love this feature and access it almost daily. If there's a fun family picture, we'll forward it on to family members to share in that memory too.

Creating online photo albums is a great way to capture special moments. You can also have them printed and made into a hardbound book for safekeeping. If you're behind on this project, start with the current year and slowly work your way backwards until you get caught up. Doing a project like this can be therapeutic and enjoyable as you relive good memories.

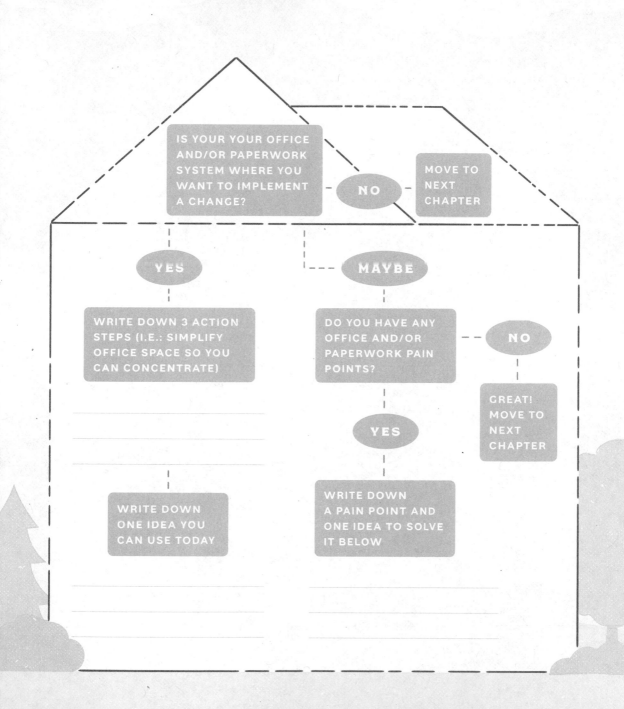

CHAPTER 16

Entryway + Mudroom

ENTRYWAYS AND MUDROOMS CAN BE PROBLEMATIC, ESPECIALLY WHEN IT comes to coat storage and shoe storage. Also, these areas usually need to pull double and triple duty. So if we're going to use these spaces for multiple purposes, it's important to make sure our systems for them are firmly in place. If they aren't, we waste space and end up being frustrated rather than proud and pleased when we walk through the door. Let's home in on how we want entryways and mudrooms to serve us and figure out the best way to make that happen.

First, let's talk about the entryway. What are your biggest stressors there? In order to decide what systems and rituals to put into place, you need to determine what is causing you stress and why you aren't loving the entryway. Once we get to the bottom of that, we'll fine-tune your systems and pair them with rituals for success.

I'll go first—following are my Pain Points in the entryway.

- Not wanting to open the coat closet for fear of something falling out
- Not enough room for coats
- No room to store extra winter gear
- No room to store nonclothing items

Write down a few things that cause you stress or are bothersome in the entryway.

_____

_____

_____

Now let's turn to the mudroom. As you did with the entryway, you need to determine *what* is causing you stress and why you aren't loving that space. You might not have a formal mudroom, but you might have a back door or a back porch that leads to your garage. Think of this space as your mudroom. If you put coats, keys, winter gear, and/or backpacks there, it's a mudroom.

Following are my Pain Points in the mudroom.

- Shoes not put away

- Coats not hung up

- Winter gear all over the place

- Dog food and dog supplies taking up space

What are your biggest stressors in the mudroom?

_____

_____

_____

Do you have a system already in place for any of the things that cause stress or are even just an annoyance in the entryway and/or mudroom? What have you tried? What do you think might work?

Systems for the Entryway + Mudroom

PAIN POINT: My Entryway Is a Jumbled Mess of Coats, Shoes, and Gear
SOLUTION: Create a Designated Place for These Items

It's easy to feel stressed out when you walk into a space and there are clothing and other items strewn everywhere. But by creating a designated space for these items, then teaching your kids how to use it, you will have one less thing to worry about. Let's break it down by item.

- Shoes. Consider the area you have and how the space is currently allotted. Is there a designated place for shoes? Or are they strewn from one end of the room to the other? One thing that helped my family is that we limit ourselves to three pairs of shoes per person in the mudroom—running shoes, dress shoes, and seasonal shoes (such as boots and flip-flops).

  If it doesn't already exist, create a place for shoes. Can you repurpose a small bookcase or shelving unit? Maybe you can use a basket or a boot tray. You can also buy a shoe organizer. Containers are an important part of the organization of this space, because without a designated home, shoes will take up space anywhere they can.

- **Coats.** Start by going through your coats and donating anything that doesn't fit or that you haven't worn in a year or more. Keep only the best and most used items.

  Then make sure there is an easy way for the coats to hang. I love wooden hangers for coats because they don't leave bumps on the shoulders and look pretty all lined up in the closet.

- **Out-of-season gear.** If you live in an area where you get to experience all four seasons, you need a place to store out-of-season gear. I use the closet in our front entryway to store winter coats and winter gear, including dress coats, mittens, gloves, hats, and scarves. We use our mudroom as our main entry and exit, so we all get to keep one or two coats there, along with the shoes we're currently wearing. Consider how you're storing these items—they're bulky and can quickly take over.

PAIN POINT: Mud in the Mudroom!

SOLUTION: Place a Sturdy Rug Outside the Door

Be ready for mud, dirt, and anything else coming in from the outside by placing a sturdy rug outside the door. I also have a decorative rug inside the door, but the sturdy rug grabs the bulk of the dirt and mud before it comes inside. Less mud, less cleaning!

PAIN POINT: Smelly Lunch Boxes Left Out Overnight

SOLUTION: Ask Kids to Unpack Lunch Boxes When They Get Home

This is such a simple thing, but I can't tell you the number of times I have gone to pack lunch in one of my children's lunch boxes only to discover the unpleasant situation waiting inside. If you teach your kids to unpack their lunch boxes as soon as they come home, it prevents any unwelcome surprises the next day. Trust me: this is worth it!

Rituals for the Entryway + Mudroom

The first place you land when you come home should be inviting. Let's add a few rituals to truly welcome you home.

Is there anything you feel is already operating as a Happy Task in the entryway and/or mudroom? Are there things you enjoy (or at least don't mind) doing when you're there? Write them down in the space below.

_____

_____

_____

SHOES OFF AT THE DOOR

This habit helps keep your floors clean and free of dirt and grime—not to mention germs. If you enjoy the feeling of going barefoot, this will be enjoyable for you. Maybe you want to grab those comfy slippers from the basket and put them on as soon as you walk in and take your shoes off. Make this a ritual with one of these simple and easy-to-implement suggestions.

HANG COATS UP

Teach this ritual early—provide hooks at an appropriate height so kids can hang up their own coats when they walk in the door.

BACKPACKS IN A CERTAIN SPOT

Place a basket or a hook next to the coats and shoes so that when kids come home they can deposit all their school stuff at the door and come in for a snack and downtime.

CREATE A PLEASANT SPACE

Simple things like a bell on the door that chimes to greet you as you walk in, a bench to sit down on when you remove your shoes, or a basket of slippers to change into all add up to a more enjoyable experience upon entry or exit.

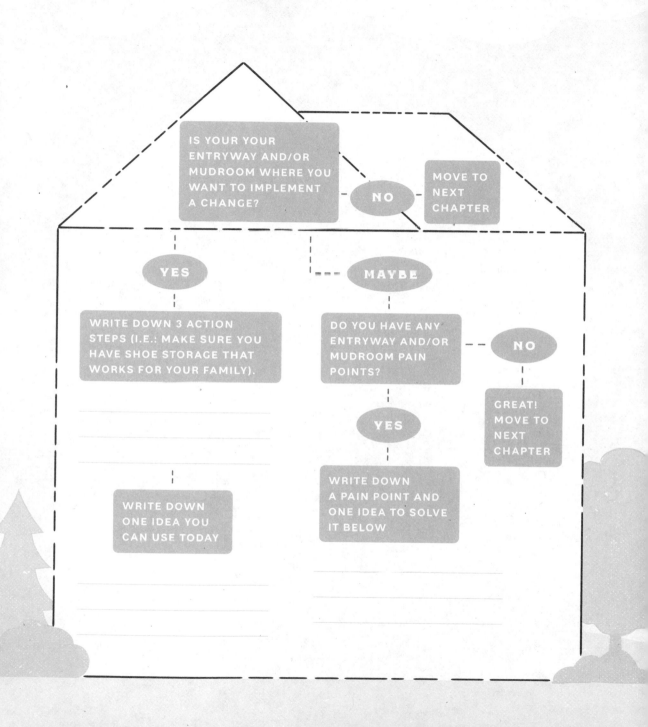

CHAPTER 17

Kids' Rooms + Spaces

TEACHING KIDS TO CLEAN THEIR ROOMS FEELS LIKE A FUTILE ENDEAVOR AT best, a war at worst. But with a little effort, you'll all be a lot happier and the room will stay consistently cleaner.

When putting a cleaning system into place with your kids, there are a few factors to consider, including:

- the ages of your children;

- how many toys and other belongings they have;

- where their toys and belongings are stored (i.e., in their bedrooms or another area);

- how much reminding and help you're okay with giving them;

- if your kids do their own laundry. My kids helped with laundry starting at age two (putting socks away, helping to "fold," and so on). Once kids are in the third or fourth grade, they can pretty much do the folding and putting away by themselves. But decide what works for you.

Ultimately, I abide by the "less is always more" principle when it comes to kids' rooms. And if you and your kids do, too, it will help them learn how to clean their rooms on their own. Keep toys, in particular, to a minimum. Too many toys are overwhelming to choose from and overwhelming to pick up. If you have a lot of toys, consider a toy library (see page 172).

Following are my Pain Points in the kids' rooms.

- Clothes not making it to hampers and baskets

- Toys and books scattered throughout the room

- Unmade beds

What are your biggest stressors in the kids' rooms?

_____

_____

_____

Do you have a system already in place for any of the things that cause stress or are even just an annoyance in the kids' rooms? What have you tried? What do you think might work?

_____

_____

_____

Systems for Kids' Rooms

"Did you clean your room?" is the age-old question to which your child always answers, "YES!". Then you go and check, and they either haven't cleaned their room the way you wanted them to, or their definition and your definition of cleaning their room are two very different things. Adding systems and pairing them with rituals will be helpful for your kids, too—and will help keep the peace around the house!

- **Teach kids to make their beds every day.** Just as it does with adults, tying a task—making the bed—to a routine will help it stick. Maybe suggest that as soon as your kids get up, they pull their beds together. Or maybe they can do it after they get dressed or brush their teeth. Spend a few weeks practicing—remember, it takes some time for new habits to stick, but once they do, they will become (mostly) automatic.

   A made bed helps give the bedroom a picked-up appearance, and it's a simple task that even preschoolers can help with. *Do not* go back and remake the beds yourself—look past it if you have to, but let the job be their own.

- **Think through your daily routine and build in tasks for your kids to take on throughout the day.** Remember chapter 4, where we looked at our morning, midday, and evening routines? Our kids have those, too, and they probably do even better than adults when it comes to working within those structures. Think through what those routines are in your house and how they might help your kids clean.

Morning. If you teach kids to make their beds every day, your kids will already be on their way to a clean room. Is there anything else you could build in during that time period—putting pajamas in the hamper, hanging bath towels up—that will make the room look even better?

Midday. If your kids are home throughout the day, is there a way to fit them into your midday routine so they can help with a room or house reset?

Evening. What is a good evening routine for your kids and their rooms? What would set them up for a peaceful night's sleep and a successful day ahead? Do they need to take a bath at night and wind down with a good book? Maybe you can read a chapter book together or they can read one on their own after they get into bed. This evening routine can be quickly turned into a ritual for your kids. Turn down their bedding, add a reading lamp and a bedside table, and they'll turn into little nighttime readers.

- **Teach "If you do this, then you get that."** Logic works with kids: "Once your bed is made and your room is picked up, then you get to choose what you do." In the summer this is easier to manage, and it's a great time to reinforce good habits. I like posting a simple task list in the kids' bedrooms—after they complete their tasks and check them off, they can choose to read, play, or maybe enjoy a little screen time.

- **Work with your kids to clean their rooms.** I know it takes time and effort for you to clean your kids' rooms with them, but it's the best way to encourage your kids to put things away where *you* want them. Learning the "right" way to clean forestalls questions and confusion in the future. This works especially well with laundry.

- **Give kids one thing to do at a time.** Like adults, kids need specific direction. If you tell your child, "Go clean your room," but when you come back in an hour it looks the same as it did before, it's probably because your directions were unclear. Unless you've taught them what a clean room should look like, they will most likely give you the deer-in-the-headlights look and be overwhelmed by the mess.

  Instead, give them very clear directions, one step at a time. For my older kids, I'll write or print out a quick checklist and put it on a clipboard for them to work through (see page 173). For my little guy, I dole out one task at a time. For example, I might hang out in the laundry room, which happens to be right outside his room, folding clothes and keeping an eye on him, ready to assist if needed. I'll say, "I'm going to be right here folding clothes. Why don't you pick up your Legos [so I don't step on them again] and tell me when you're done?" Then when he's done, I'll say, "Great job—that looks so much better. Can you pick up your books, too? Then we can head outside and have fun." One thing at a time is so much easier for everyone.

- **Use a timer to make cleaning a game.** Using a timer can turn quick cleaning sessions into a game. Race the timer and do a quick before-meal pickup, or just set it for five minutes and see what you can get done in that little spurt. Put on music and make it fun. If you have little ones, they can help, too. They'll need assistance, but they can definitely learn to put their toys back. Make it quick and simple. Start with five or ten minutes to hold their attention.

- **Have cleaning supplies handy.** Kids like to clean with real tools. If you want them to dust their rooms, give them dusters. If they're able to vacuum, let them. Keep a small cleaning caddy in their rooms—this works especially well with little ones. Even baby wipes can be used for cleaning!

Having kids is another great reason to switch to all-natural cleaning products if you haven't already. You'll feel better knowing that you can leave your kids to clean their spaces without worrying about what they're touching.

PAIN POINT: My Kids Have Too Many Toys—They're Everywhere!

SOLUTION: Toy Library

A toy library is the perfect storage solution for toddlers and preschool-age kids. The premise is that you store all the toys by type in bins. Convert a closet, use part of a child's closet, corner off an area in the basement—establish your library anywhere you can stash some lidded bins. Label the bins and put them on rotation: keep most of the toys put away and pull out one to three bins at a time. This keeps toys and choices fresh and ensures that kids will play more deeply and longer when they have fewer toys and fewer choices to make. If this sounds strange, try it for a week and see how differently your kids play.

PAIN POINT: The Kids' Spaces Are Always a Disaster by the End of the Day

SOLUTION: Teach Your Kids to Clean as They Go

Be intentional throughout the day—it's always easier to tidy up as you go rather than clean everything up at the end of the day, and it's a great habit to teach kids.

When our kids were little, we reset the area where they were playing multiple times a day. This helped them learn to clean up as they go, and it was so much easier to clean up a little instead of a lot. Kids like to be involved in cleaning. The same principle applies to the entire home: as you're preparing dinner, put the prep dishes in the dishwasher; as you're getting ready for the day, put your toiletries away instead of leaving them on the bathroom counter.

Whatever works for your family, be consistent in making that happen. For example, if it's helpful to do a quick cleanup before your kids' rest time or nap time every day, spend the five to ten minutes that it takes to do it. Being consistent helps build habits, and it makes it easier to clean up when you're doing it regularly.

What types of tasks would go on a room-cleanup list for your kids? Write them down in the space below.

_____

_____

_____

Rituals for Kids' Rooms

Is there anything you feel is already operating as a Happy Task in your kids' rooms? Are there things you enjoy (or at least don't mind) doing when you're there? Write them down in the space below.

_____

_____

_____

WHEN THE HOUSE IS CLEAN . . . GET OUT!

When our two older kids were little, we'd do a quick cleanup of their rooms and play spaces, then head out to the park for a picnic lunch and more play time. This did us all good—fresh air, sunshine, and a walk. In inclement weather we'd head to the library or I'd take the stroller to the mall and just walk around. Then it was back home for naps and a little quiet time for me. If you're working outside the home, you can do this after dinner.

SIT BACK AND ENJOY

Relaxing and enjoying your hard work is hard even for adults to do. So at my house, the kids and I will play a game or watch a movie after everything is picked up. It's quality time spent together, and we can all enjoy the clean house a little longer.

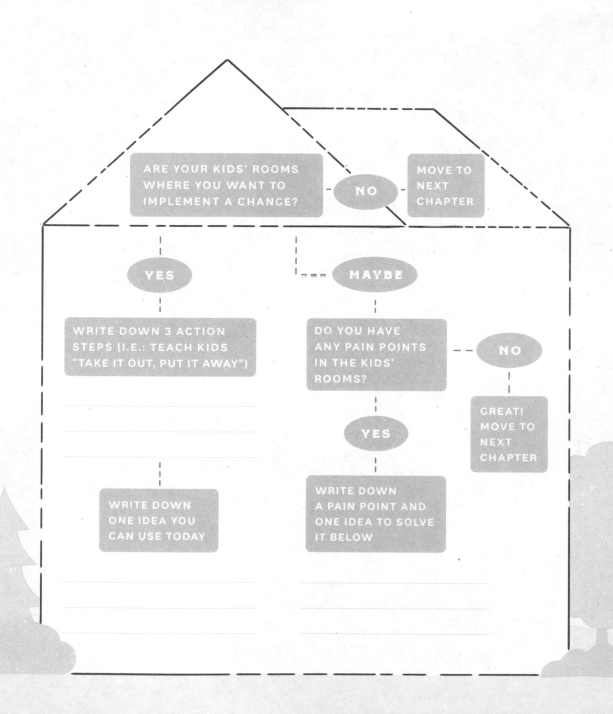

ARE YOUR KIDS' ROOMS WHERE YOU WANT TO IMPLEMENT A CHANGE?

NO

MOVE TO NEXT CHAPTER

YES

MAYBE

WRITE DOWN 3 ACTION STEPS (I.E.: TEACH KIDS "TAKE IT OUT, PUT IT AWAY")

DO YOU HAVE ANY PAIN POINTS IN THE KIDS' ROOMS?

NO

GREAT! MOVE TO NEXT CHAPTER

YES

WRITE DOWN ONE IDEA YOU CAN USE TODAY

WRITE DOWN A PAIN POINT AND ONE IDEA TO SOLVE IT BELOW

CHAPTER 18

Garage + Storage

LET ME START BY SAYING THAT THE GARAGE AND STORAGE AREAS ARE MY nemeses. These spaces are difficult: they get messy and dirty and are easy to ignore and put off cleaning. They hold extra stuff that we're not 100 percent ready to let go of quite yet and stuff that we've probably forgotten about. I'll join with you here: together, let's commit to finally conquering these dreaded tasks. Whether we're talking about a crawl space, a closet, a one-car garage, or a four-car garage, there are systems we can put to work for us in these overlooked and avoided areas.

Garage Stressors and Pain Point Tasks

What are your garage and storage stressors? Is there a lingering odor in your closet? Is your car a dumping ground? Is your garage littered with projects and supplies—a mess that doesn't seem to have a beginning or an end?

In order to decide what systems and rituals to put into place in your garage and storage areas, you need to determine *what* is causing you stress and why you aren't loving these spaces. Once we get to the bottom of that, we'll fine-tune your expectations and determine what can be done.

I'll go first—following are my Pain Points in the garage.

- Toys and sports equipment all over even though there's storage for everything

- Empty boxes that need to be recycled

- Using the garage as a dumping ground for things we don't want inside

Following are my Pain Points in the storage areas (in our house, this is also known as the basement).

- Not everything is mine—some is my husband's from childhood; some is mine from childhood; some is kid stuff; some is stuff that I just haven't looked at since we moved, more than ten years ago

- It feels overwhelming and all-consuming

- It's an unfinished basement, so there's really no reason to keep it clean and tidy

Write down some of your own Pain Points—things that cause you stress or are bothersome in the garage and storage areas. Do you have a system already in place for any of the things that cause stress or are even just an annoyance in the garage or your storage areas? What have you tried? What do you think might work?

PAIN POINT: I'm Too Overwhelmed; I Don't Know Where to Start

SOLUTION: Break the Task Down into Small, Actionable Chunks

You don't need to go through everything all at once! In fact, if you break the task down into small chunks, you'll feel a sense of accomplishment when you get each one of the chunks done, giving you motivation to keep going.

Using masking tape, mark off a small area of the floor—four feet by four feet works well for me—and concentrate on whatever lies within its bounds. Or go through one box per day, the goal being to consolidate what you want to keep and get rid of what you no longer need.

PAIN POINT: I Need to Get Rid of Stuff

SOLUTION: Participate in a Neighborhood Garage Sale

If you need to get rid of stuff and are finding it hard to get motivated, participating in or initiating a neighborhood garage sale might be a good motivator. There are several advantages to this: you'll have to leave your garage door open, giving you a reason to get the space organized; you'll have to establish an end date for your decluttering; and you'll earn some cash.

Below are some tips for preparing for a garage sale.

- Set up a regular time to hold the event—yearly or more often, if you like.

- Prepare for the event by decluttering throughout the year. Maybe you can do it when you have some time off around the holidays. Maybe you prefer to do

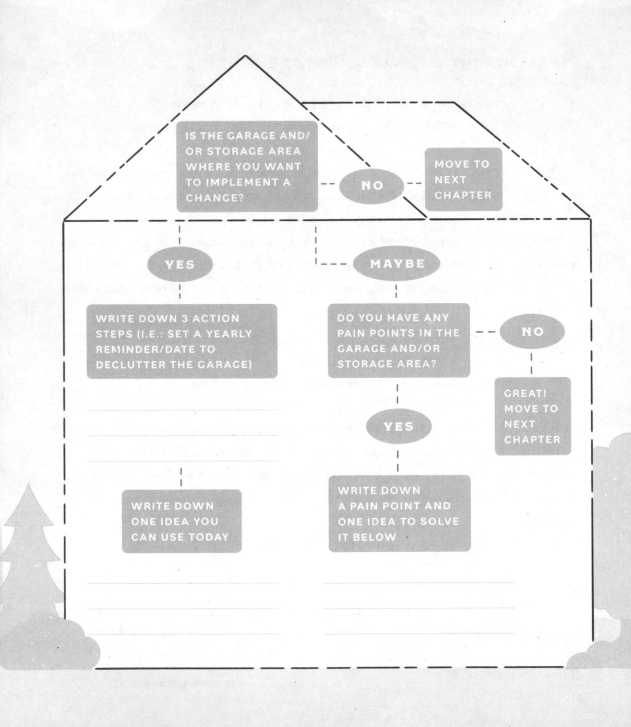

IS THE GARAGE AND/OR STORAGE AREA WHERE YOU WANT TO IMPLEMENT A CHANGE?

NO

MOVE TO NEXT CHAPTER

YES

MAYBE

WRITE DOWN 3 ACTION STEPS (I.E.: SET A YEARLY REMINDER/DATE TO DECLUTTER THE GARAGE)

DO YOU HAVE ANY PAIN POINTS IN THE GARAGE AND/OR STORAGE AREA?

NO

GREAT! MOVE TO NEXT CHAPTER

YES

WRITE DOWN ONE IDEA YOU CAN USE TODAY

WRITE DOWN A PAIN POINT AND ONE IDEA TO SOLVE IT BELOW

a thorough spring cleaning, or maybe you can enlist your kids to help you over the summer.

- Do a quick declutter daily.

- Unsure of what to keep? Put items that you *might* want to keep in a box. Put a date on it—anywhere from one month to one year in the future. When that date arrives, if you didn't think about, wonder about, need, or use the items in that box, just take it directly to your local donation center.

- Keep a donation bin handy and use it whenever you get the time to sort and purge.

PAIN POINT: **Toys and Sports Equipment Are Strewn All Over**
SOLUTION: **Keep Everything Organized**

Get creative with your storage. Add hooks to your garage walls for things like tennis rackets, hockey sticks, ice skates, baseball mitts, etc. You can make it fun by tracing these items on the wall so they always get hung up in their proper places. Kids will love to put the "puzzle pieces" back on the walls! Reuse empty bins and appropriate shelves and lockers. Group like items together, toss or donate what you no longer use or need, and get your storage space back to organized bliss.

Rituals for Garage + Storage Spaces

Even though it doesn't feel like cleaning up the garage and storage areas could possibly be enjoyable, if you involve your family and make it fun, the event might just be a special memory in the making.

Is there anything you feel is already operating as a Happy Task in your garage or storage spaces? Are there things you enjoy (or at least don't mind) doing when you're there? Write them down in the space below.

_____

_____

_____

_____

FAMILY CLEANING DAYS

Maybe by now you've caught on to my trick: when you get other people involved, cleaning not only gets done faster, it's also more enjoyable! So get everyone into the act. Block out time on the calendar to tackle these neglected spaces—cue the music, order pizza, and get it done!

When our kids were really little, we would bring them to the basement with us, and they would ride their toy cars and trikes while we sorted and purged. A similar method works well when cleaning out a garage if the weather cooperates. Sidewalk chalk, bubble bottles, strollers, and bikes usually occupy little ones while you're going through your stuff.

Give older kids a box of toys to sort through. They may find some gems to add back to their toy library or decide that some of them are ready to be tossed or donated. Enlist their help with watching the younger kids—they can keep them on task or play with them while you're sorting and purging.

CHAPTER 19

Vehicles

I REALIZE THAT VEHICLES AREN'T TECHNICALLY PART OF OUR HOMES, BUT they are often extensions of our homes—getting us to work, getting kids to school and soccer practice—and as such they can become a dumping ground for crumbs and papers, making it more stressful than necessary to get from point A to point B.

What are your stressors when it comes to your vehicles? Is there a lingering odor? Are there crumbs on the seats? Do you feel stressed out just getting into your car? I like a clean car, but it's difficult when you have two dogs and three kids and when your vehicle is the family vehicle.

Following are my vehicle Pain Points .

- Kids' stuff left in the car—socks, shoes, glasses, books, food remnants

- Receipts left in the car (this one's on me)

- Car windows are hard to clean on the inside, and they are smudged up by the dogs or kids right after they are cleaned.

Write down a few things that cause you stress or are bothersome in your vehicle. Do you have a system in place for doing any of the things that cause stress or even for those that are just an annoyance in your vehicle? What have you tried? What do you think might work?

Systems for Vehicles

PAIN POINT: My Car Has Become a Dumping Ground
SOLUTION: Keep a Garbage Bag in the Car

This is super simple to implement. Expect that there will be trash in the car and have a receptacle in place for it. Hang a plastic bag from a headrest or put a small garbage bin on the floor behind the front seats. Teach passengers what it's for and empty it regularly.

PAIN POINT: I Can't Keep the Inside of My Car Clean
SOLUTION: Plan for the Mess

If you are in your car constantly, it can definitely get cluttered and dirty in a hurry. Here are some simple solutions to keep it clean:

- Keep a roll of paper towels and/or baby wipes in the car. I've had a few puking-in-the-car incidents with kids and dogs, and these were a godsend in those very messy moments.

- Make a "no food in the car" rule. I know this is hard, but all it takes is one milk spill and you'll agree with me. It'll cut down the time you spend cleaning the inside of your car dramatically.

- Keep a microfiber cloth or duster in the car and wipe the dashboard while you're waiting in a drive-through line, waiting to pick up your kids, and any other time when the car is in park and you don't have to concentrate on the road.

- Rubber floor mats are a game changer. I highly recommend them.

- Take the trash with you whenever you get out of the car.

PAIN POINT: Kids Always Leave Stuff in the Car
SOLUTION: Quick Car Check

Take a minute before getting out of the car to do a quick car check—ask the kids if they've left anything in the car and do a floor and seat check as they get out.

Rituals for Vehicles

Is there anything you feel is already operating as a Happy Task when it comes to your vehicles? Things you enjoy (or at least don't mind) doing for them? Write them down in the space below.

Following are some rituals you can initiate to make your car a more enjoyable place to spend time.

- Take your car through the car wash every time you fill up with gas—or at least once a month. Tying this ritual to something you normally do (getting gas) will help you feel like there's less to do the next time you get in it.

- Keep a book and/or a notebook and pen in your purse or in the glove compartment so you have something to do when you're stuck waiting.

- Treat yourself to a professional car detailing every once in a while. When the car feels sparkly clean, you'll be motivated to keep it that way!

- Kids love washing cars! Make it an event—they can help wash, vacuum, and clean out the mess. Especially on a hot summer day, what's better than a sudsy, wet wash to keep them entertained?

- If you are in the car a lot, consider something special to listen to like a special Spotify playlist, favorite podcast, or a subscription to satellite radio.

CAR TIME IS QUALITY TIME WITH KIDS

One huge benefit of spending time in the car is that it gives you quality time with your kids. You can have conversations with them before or after school or before or after practice. You can listen to an audiobook, put on your favorite music, or play a game (such as Who Am I?, the license plate game, and others). Think of your clean and happy car as a place for connection.

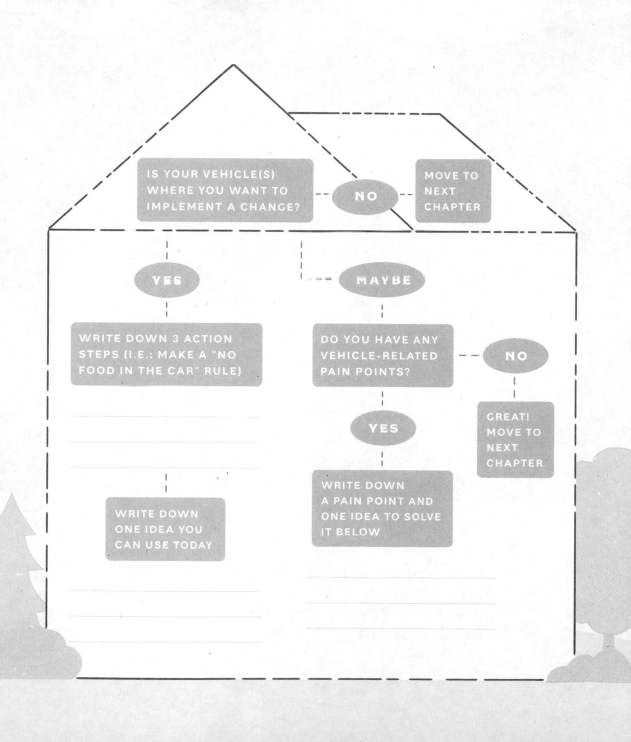

CHAPTER 20

Cleaning Routine

I WROTE ABOUT A CLEAN-HOME ROUTINE FOR ANY SCHEDULE IN CHAPTER 5, but this is where you get to fine-tune and really think about *your* cleaning routine—what cleaning you do, how it fits into your life, how you can make it more enjoyable, and how it can take less time. I love figuring out the best way to clean something quickly and safely and am eager for you to dive into this part of the book so you can establish the systems and rituals that will keep your home sparkly clean!

Start by letting go of any misconceptions you have about cleaning—thoughts such as "It's just going to get messy again—what's the point?" and "I'll clean when my kids are grown; I'm enjoying them right now." The fact of the matter is, if you're cleaning a little bit every day, your home will be clean most of the time. You'll have less stress, feel less overwhelmed by clutter, and be able to enjoy your life.

There is no judgment here about what the current state of your home is or what your cleaning routine—or lack thereof—looks like. I have lots of readers who have followed me for years without doing the Clean Mama routine. But when they finally come around to trying it, they tell me that they didn't realize it was so easy and that it will actually keep their homes clean.

What are your biggest cleaning-routine stressors? In order to decide what systems and rituals to put into place in your cleaning routine, you need to determine *what* is causing you stress and why you aren't loving or even sort of enjoying this practice. Once we get to the bottom of that, we'll fine-tune your systems and pair them with rituals for success.

I'll go first—following are my cleaning-routine Pain Points (yes, I have them too!).

- Lack of time

- Frustration with the messes made by others

- I am easily overwhelmed

- Laundry

Write down a few things that cause you stress when it comes to your cleaning routine.

_____

_____

_____

Systems for Cleaning

A cleaning routine is a system. It can be organized, methodical, and enjoyable. Even though all cleaning tasks might not be super fun for you, think of that feeling you have when you walk into a room and know that everything that can be done on that day has been done. Or maybe you didn't finish cleaning the bathrooms, but you know you can catch up on your catchall day. There is an odd sense of freedom when you know what to clean and when to clean it.

Don't skip this part of the book: now that you've decluttered your home and created systems and rituals around your Happy Tasks and Pain Point Tasks, it's time to give your cleaning routine a little attention.

A cleaning routine for someone who works out of the house all day will look different from a cleaning routine for someone who's home with the little ones all day. The two routines will call for completing tasks at different times and require varying amounts of time and energy. They will also vary based on the size of the home and what needs to be cleaned. Maybe you have a cleaning crew who comes every other week—you still need a cleaning routine to deal with the stuff that accumulates daily. Let's give it some thought.

DAILY CLEANING ROUTINE

We covered this in chapter 5, but as a reminder, below are my daily cleaning tasks, the five things I try to do every day.

- Make beds
- Check floors
- Wipe counters
- Declutter
- Do laundry

Write down your current daily cleaning routine—the things you do daily.

What is working in your daily cleaning routine?

What isn't working in your daily cleaning routine?

What is your ideal daily cleaning routine?

What is the best time of day for you to go through your daily cleaning routine?

Again, following are my weekly cleaning tasks—I have them organized according to days of the week and zones. Instead of setting aside a day for each room, I set aside days for each task—clean bathrooms, dust the house, vacuum all the floors, wash all the floors. As you're thinking about your own weekly cleaning routine, think about how you want to structure these tasks.

- Monday: Bathroom cleaning day
- Tuesday: Dusting day
- Wednesday: Vacuuming day
- Thursday: Floor washing day

- Friday: Catch-all day
- Saturday: Sheets and towels day
- Sunday: Just the daily tasks

Write down your current weekly cleaning routine—the things you do weekly.

What is working in your weekly cleaning routine?

What isn't working in your weekly cleaning routine?

_____

_____

_____

_____

What is your ideal weekly cleaning routine?

_____

_____

_____

_____

What is the best time of day for you to go through your weekly cleaning routine? Does this vary by the day of the week or by task?

_____

_____

_____

_____

ROTATING CLEANING ROUTINE

I consider deep-cleaning tasks to be a rotating cleaning routine. There is a time and place for them, but it isn't daily or weekly. Plug these in when you feel confident in your daily and weekly cleaning routines. If this feels overwhelming, brainstorm some ideas and come back to it later.

Following are the tasks that I complete on a monthly, bimonthly, or quarterly basis.

- Vacuum and wash baseboards
- Clean light fixtures in each room of the house
- Wash rugs
- Launder pillows, blankets, and comforters
- Clean oven
- Clean appliances
- Clean fridge and freezer
- Polish wood furniture
- Spot-clean walls

- Spot-clean and vacuum upholstered furniture
- Rotate and vacuum mattresses
- Wash windows
- Clean carpets
- Clean large appliances like air conditioners (leave this to the pros); replace filters in the furnace, humidifier, air cleaner (if you have one), dehumidifier, and vacuum cleaner
- Clean wall switches, desktop phones, and remotes

Write down your current rotating cleaning routine—the things you do monthly, bimonthly, or quarterly.

_____

_____

_____

_____

What is working in your rotating cleaning routine?

What isn't working in your rotating cleaning routine?

What is your ideal rotating cleaning routine?

When is the best time for you to go through your rotating cleaning routine?

Rituals for Cleaning

We often think of cleaning as a chore, and sometimes it is, but we can add elements that make it enjoyable. Try a few of these ideas and see if they help.

Before we get started, is there anything you feel is already operating as a Happy Task when it comes to your cleaning routine? What parts of the cleaning routine do you enjoy (or at least don't mind) doing? Write them down in the space below.

MAKING CLEANING SOLUTIONS

The process of making cleaning solutions is so satisfying for me. When I do it myself, there are several advantages: I know what I'm cleaning with; I've formulated hundreds of recipes that *work*, so I have a lot to choose from; I don't have to go to the store when I need a bottle of glass cleaning spray; and it's so economical! See the appendix for my favorite cleaning solution recipes. This ritual might be what turns you on to a cleaning routine: truly, when you make your own products, it is so much more enjoyable!

BUY IN BULK

I buy the ingredients for my homemade cleaning products in bulk. When I get them home, I decant them into labeled containers and keep them on a turntable in my cleaning closet. When I want to mix a batch of something, I combine the necessary ingredients from the closet into a smaller dispenser or spray bottle and clean away.

USE A CLEANING CADDY

A cleaning caddy is a system, but it can feel like a ritual if you use products you enjoy. (See the appendix for easy recipes to make your own cleaning products.) Get a functional bucket or compartmentalized bin with a handle and outfit it with your favorite cleaning supplies. I love the color aqua, so I fill my caddy with white and aqua containers and tools. Just using products I think are cute makes cleaning less of a chore.

A cleaning caddy needs the following four components:

- a spray,
- a scrub,
- tools, and
- cleaning cloths.

Think of these four ingredients as your building blocks. You need a spray to wet your surfaces; a scrub for those hard-to-clean spots; tools, such as scrub brushes and squeegees; and cleaning cloths to wipe the surfaces (see page 98). Simple, right?

DESIGNATE A SPECIFIC TIME OF THE DAY FOR CLEANING

Instead of waiting for that perfect pocket of cleaning time to open up, set a specific time of day for cleaning. This is schedule-dependent, but if you tend to not get anything done after 9:00 a.m., try to do a bit of cleaning from 8:00 to 8:30 every morning.

REWARD YOURSELF

Sometimes it helps to give yourself a little reward after you've completed a task that feels like a chore. After you finish cleaning the bathroom, for example, sit down and read a magazine. Or light a candle. Or pour yourself a second cup of coffee. You deserve it!

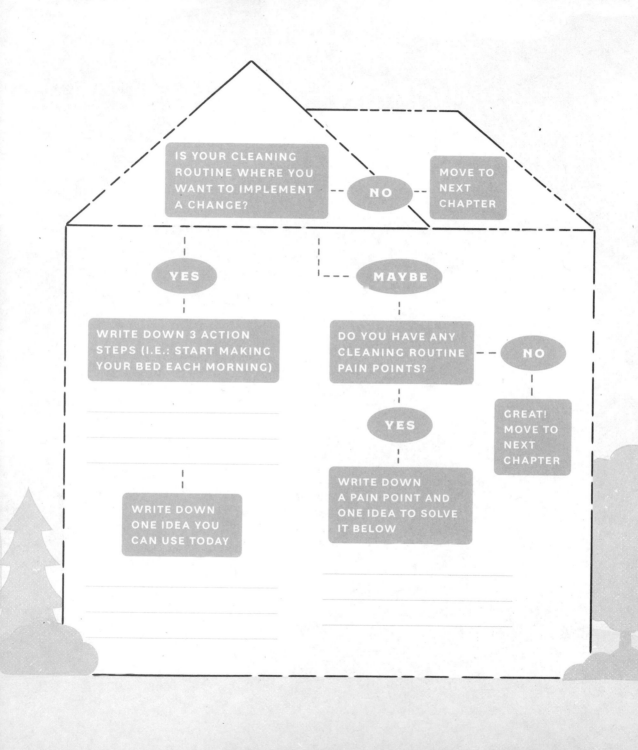

IS YOUR CLEANING ROUTINE WHERE YOU WANT TO IMPLEMENT A CHANGE?

NO

MOVE TO NEXT CHAPTER

YES

MAYBE

WRITE DOWN 3 ACTION STEPS (I.E.: START MAKING YOUR BED EACH MORNING)

DO YOU HAVE ANY CLEANING ROUTINE PAIN POINTS?

NO

GREAT! MOVE TO NEXT CHAPTER

YES

WRITE DOWN ONE IDEA YOU CAN USE TODAY

WRITE DOWN A PAIN POINT AND ONE IDEA TO SOLVE IT BELOW

CHAPTER 21

Whole-House Clutter Catchers

EVEN WITH THE BEST SYSTEMS IN PLACE, IT'S STILL EASY FOR CLUTTER TO take over. Getting rid of clutter is all about finding solutions, which I call clutter catchers. For example, if the problem is that towels are on the floor in the bathroom, perhaps it's because there isn't a hook where people can hang them. Put a hook up, and you've easily solved the problem. Are your kids' backpacks strewn from one end of the mudroom to the other? Put a basket in the corner where kids can drop their backpacks and lunch boxes when they get home from school.

I found that after I implemented a whole-house clutter-catcher system, our home stays relatively orderly throughout the week. Look at the suggestions below and pick one or two to try. Again, don't try to tackle them all right now, but ask yourself whether there are any areas of your home that are usually more cluttered than others. Write your answers below and keep them in mind as you look through the list that follows.

I recommend starting with the following six whole-house clutter catchers.

- **Command center with a family calendar.** This can be where you keep important dates, school and sports schedules, permission slips, and other items.

- **Filing cabinet with hanging file folders.** This can be where you keep your children's schoolwork and papers—see chapter 15 for more ideas.

- **In and out baskets.** This simple system, which separates what you need to deal with (in) from what you need to file or mail (out), is really all you need to get a handle on dealing with your paperwork daily.

- **A place for keys.** This can be a hook, a place in your command center, or a bowl, but the main thing is to establish a location and use it consistently. You'll know where your keys are, and so will everyone else in your home.

- **Small laundry basket for each family member.** There's no point in having a monster hamper—keep the loads manageable, and it'll be easier for whoever is doing the laundry.

- **Donation basket (or box or bin).** After you've done your decluttering, set up a permanent spot for donations in your home. Teach your family members what goes in the container, and once it fills up, take it to your favorite drop-off spot. If you have kids you're saving clothing for, place the clothes your other kids have outgrown in a bin. Label it with the appropriate size, and when it's full, put it in storage or pass it down.

Below are more of my favorite whole-house clutter catchers: think about which ones you can put in place. Even the littlest thing can make a big difference!

- **Hooks for anything that needs hanging.** Brooms, towels, dusting wands, coats, robes . . . I'm a big fan of adhesive, removable hooks that can be relocated if I decide I want to put them somewhere else. I even use a hook on the back of the under-the-kitchen-sink cabinet door for drying damp bar mop towels.

- **Basket for dirty cleaning cloths.** Put a small metal basket, or any ventilated container, under the sink for dirty (but dry) dish cloths, hand towels, and cleaning cloths. When the basket is full, toss the cloths in the washing machine. Keep like cloths together—for example, don't wash microfiber with other materials.

- **"On your way up" basket.** This is where I collect things throughout the day that need to be taken upstairs or anywhere else in the house. Try it! As you find clutter in one area of your home, put it in the basket, and at the end of the day put those items back where they belong. It maximizes efficiency (you're not having to make multiple trips up the stairs to put things away) and cuts down on mess throughout the house.

- **Daily drawer.** Designate a drawer for things you use daily—this can be in a bathroom, in the kitchen, in the office, or in a bedroom. For example, if this is in your bathroom, it's for your toothbrush, toothpaste, contacts, glasses, etc. Things you use every day are kept easily accessible and at the ready. If you don't have a drawer, use counter storage for these items.

- **Zone containers.** Every time you embark on a cleaning project in a room or a particular space, divide it into zones in your mind. Group like items, or items you use during a specific time of the day, together in those zones. These zones will guide you as you figure out the best way to put new systems in place. Following are some examples.

  - File box for kids' important papers + memorabilia

  - Magazine basket

  - Lunch-packing station. Keep the lunch-making supplies in one spot: sandwich bags, water bottles, storage containers, etc.

  - Smoothie-making caddy. Keep the powders and add-ins in one spot.

  - Cereal bin. Remove the inner bags from cereal boxes, fold over the tops of the bags, and use clothespins or clips to hold them closed. Then put the various bags in a bin. This saves time and allows the kiddos to grab their own cereal—yay!

  - Coffee corner. For your coffeepot, coffee, mugs, spoons, and anything else you need to make your daily cup.

  - Container, basket, or bag for reusable shopping bags and insulated totes

  - Sink trays for hand soap and dish soap dispensers. This makes your sink look neater, keeps drips on the tray, and makes cleaning the counters easier.

  - Tray or basket for makeup and toiletries

  - Eye-care drawer. For glasses and contact lenses in the bathroom.

- Baskets or trays for shoes and boots

- Compartmentalized plastic box with a lid for battery storage. Bonus points if you keep a small screwdriver in the box for quick battery changes.

- Charging station for phones and tablets. Keep them out of the bedrooms, and keep those cords untangled.

- Container for charging and other cords that aren't used daily (label them first)

Make a list below of whole-house clutter catchers that would be helpful in your home.

_____

_____

_____

Do you have a clutter-catching system in place that you want to refine?

_____

_____

_____

CHAPTER 22

A Final Note

THOUGH WE'VE REACHED THE END OF THIS BOOK, THIS IS JUST THE BEGINNING of your journey to home bliss. Every system and ritual you try, every Pain Point Task you pair with a Happy Task, brings you closer to having a home that you want to be in and that you want to welcome others into.

Don't believe for a second that perfection is the end goal. It's not. Don't get caught in the lie that if your home is bigger, better, cleaner, more organized, fill in the blank . . . *then* you'll be happy and fulfilled. We all know how that goes! Embrace the mess! Enjoy where you are and find a better way to love your home and the time you spend there. A perfectly curated life is not what you want. Rather, you want a cozy home that exudes warmth and welcome. Simple systems and rituals give way to calm and order in a natural, comfortable way.

My hope is that as you put some of these systems and rituals into place, you will be able to walk into your home after an exhausting day and feel a sense of peace. Your house will become a haven, one that you've worked on and refined—a perfectly imperfect place where you want to spend time. Take it slow, bask in each little win, and calm your soul. You are creating a sanctuary for yourself and those you love, and the time spent will help you discover an appreciation for your home that you didn't know existed.

Welcome home.

Clean Mama's Tried-and-True Recipes

I make most of my own cleaning products. I like knowing what's in them, and I like being able to mix up a cleaner whenever I need one. Below are recipes for the cleaners I stock in my cleaning caddies.

Refer back to this section as you're decluttering and cleaning—I bet you'll find a handful of new favorite recipes to try. Happy cleaning!

STONE-CLEANING SPRAY

This gentle yet effective spray also makes a great all-purpose cleaner. Use it to clean your sealed stone (marble, granite, quartz) counters.

INGREDIENTS

1½ cups water

2 tablespoons rubbing alcohol

¼ teaspoon liquid castile soap or dish soap

SPECIAL EQUIPMENT

16-ounce spray bottle

Soft cleaning cloth

Combine all ingredients in the spray bottle, spray on surfaces, and wipe clean with the cloth.

GLASS-CLEANING SPRAY

Looking for clean, streak-free windows and mirrors? This quick-drying spray will do the trick!

INGREDIENTS

1½ cups water

1½ tablespoons white vinegar

1½ tablespoons rubbing alcohol

3 drops peppermint essential oil

SPECIAL EQUIPMENT

16-ounce spray bottle

Soft cleaning cloth

Combine all ingredients in the spray bottle. To clean mirrors, spray the solution on the cleaning cloth; to clean windows, spray the solution directly on the glass. Wipe to a streak-free shine.

ALL-PURPOSE DISINFECTING SPRAY

Use this spray in bathrooms and the kitchen—anywhere that needs a little cleaning boost. Do not, however, use it on stone surfaces.

INGREDIENTS

1¼ cups water

¼ cup white vinegar

¼ cup vodka or rubbing alcohol

15 drops essential oil of your choice

SPECIAL EQUIPMENT

16-ounce spray bottle

Soft cleaning cloth

Combine all ingredients in the spray bottle, spray liberally on surfaces, and wipe clean with the cloth.

ALL-PURPOSE SPRAY

This the perfect clean-just-about-anywhere spray. Want the kids to help? Hand them a bottle of this. But do not use it on stone surfaces.

INGREDIENTS

1¼ cups water

½ cup white vinegar

10 drops essential oil of your choice

SPECIAL EQUIPMENT

16-ounce spray bottle

Soft cleaning cloth

Combine all ingredients in the spray bottle, spray liberally on surfaces, and wipe clean with the cloth.

FLOOR-CLEANING SPRAY

Need a gentle and effective floor-cleaning spray? Try this on any type of floor. You can also pour it directly into the container of a spray mop if you don't want to carry the bottle around with you.

INGREDIENTS

1¾ cups warm water

1 to 2 drops liquid castile soap

3 to 5 drops essential oil of your choice (optional)

SPECIAL EQUIPMENT

16-ounce spray bottle

Combine all ingredients in the spray bottle. Spray on small sections of the floor at a time, then mop and admire your clean floors.

SHOWER SPRAY

Looking for a way to prevent soap scum and mildew from forming? Spray this on the tile and glass right after showering and you'll spend less time scrubbing on bathroom cleaning day.

INGREDIENTS

½ cup vodka or rubbing alcohol

1 cup water

10 drops peppermint essential oil

SPECIAL EQUIPMENT

16-ounce spray bottle

Squeegee

Combine all ingredients in the spray bottle. Spray the shower or tub immediately after showering. Wipe with a squeegee to remove excess water and prevent water spots (no rinsing necessary).

NIGHTLY SINK SCRUB

After the dishes are done for the night, using a nightly sink scrub in your sink will leave the surface sparkling clean. See page 79 for the recipe.

FABRIC REFRESHER

Looking for a safe and effective fabric refresher that eliminates odors and works well on bedding and pillows? See page 111 for the recipe.

BATHROOM SCRUB

Sprinkle this scrub anywhere in the bathroom where you need a little extra cleaning power. It's perfect for the tub, shower, sink, and faucets.

INGREDIENTS

2 cups baking soda

20 drops essential oil of your choice

1 squirt liquid castile soap

SPECIAL EQUIPMENT

Container with a lid or shaker top

Scrub brush or sponge

Pour the baking soda into your container. (I like using a mason jar.) Drop the essential oil on top of the baking soda and stir with a table knife to combine.

Wet your surfaces and sprinkle the scrub liberally on top. Squirt with castile soap and scrub with the scrub brush or sponge. Rinse thoroughly.

Store the baking soda mixture under the sink; it will keep for several months.

"BEFORE YOU GO" SPRAY

You know that "before you go" spray you've seen in the store? You can make your own with just four ingredients. See page 102 for the recipe.

SOFT CLEANING PASTE

Sometimes you need a little extra *oomph* to tackle those tough-to-clean spots such as ovens, tile, and grout. This paste gives you the power you need! Grab your scrub brush and a scoop of this scrub and you'll be looking for things to clean.

INGREDIENTS

1 cup baking soda

½ cup washing soda (such as Arm & Hammer)

1 teaspoon citric acid

1 tablespoon kosher salt

4 tablespoons liquid castile soap

20 drops essential oil of your choice

½ to ¾ cup white vinegar

SPECIAL EQUIPMENT

Sealed nonreactive container for storage

Scrub brush or sponge

Combine baking soda, washing soda, citric acid*, and salt in a large nonreactive bowl. Add soap and essential oil and stir to combine. Carefully add ½ cup vinegar (the mixture will bubble). Mix thoroughly, adding more vinegar if needed to make the paste hold together. Scoop out a tablespoon or two and apply with the scrub brush or sponge. Rinse thoroughly. Store in a sealed nonreactive container.

*Citric acid is usually available in the canning section of the supermarket.

INDEX